# The New SAP Blue Book
A Concise Business Guide to the World of SAP

# The New SAP Blue Book

A Concise Business Guide to the World of SAP

Michael Doane
with Paul Reynolds and Michael Connor

# The SAP Blue Book

This book was written by Michael Doane.

Published by Michael Doane

Printed in the United States.

ISBN: 978-1-57579-342-9

# CONTENTS

# Acknowledgments

While I remain deeply grateful to the many people who provided counsel and content to the original SAP Blue Book, it is time to acknowledge those who have contributed wisdom and insight to the New SAP Blue Book.

Beyond Paul Reynolds and Mike Connor who contribute chapters to this version, I wish to thank David Yockelson, Kip Martin, Dane Anderson, and Stan Lepeak, all from the now extinct META Group, as well as Mark Dendinger, Joshua Greenbaum, Bruce Blitch, and Jon Reed.

If you come to a fork in the road, take it.
Yogi Berra


I didn't say all the things I said.
Yogi Berra

# PREFACE

Years ago, I was the IT manager for Europe for a major English electronics and defense firm. Monthly meetings were held in Brussels, including managing directors and finance directors. At each meeting, I was afforded one half hour to report progress for our European wide systems implementation and I noted that once the subject turned from commercial and financial subjects to 'computers', half of my audience immediately went into *the zone* and I was only surprised not to hear outright snoring.

The same reaction often occurs with senior managers at firms that are considering SAP. The misconception is that it is a computer subject, when in reality it is very much a business subject. The consequence of this misconception is that many firms have failed to implement and use SAP software because of management presumptions that it is just the current hot software and that it should be implemented just as other software has been implemented.

The first version of this book appeared early in 1998. This is the sixth updated version as SAP, its ecosystem, and its clients have all continued to make vast strides, thus changing the advisory landscape.

Earlier versions of this book were, necessarily, quite cautionary as the period dating from the arrival of SAP R/3 through to the new millennium was relatively a maturing period during which many firms, especially those in the Global 2000, struggled mightily to implement and properly deploy SAP software.

My perspective in regard to SAP has evolved through the years. From 1995 through 2000, I was an SAP practice leader, helping clients acquire and implement SAP R/3. Through those years, my focus was upon the best and fastest ways to implement while still setting up a client for measurable business benefit. For the past six years, however, I have worked as an industry analyst with a focus on systems integration and enterprise applications strategies. This work has included a number of research projects addressing the best (and worst) practices for enterprise applications implementations as well as post-implementation strategies. In my four plus years at META Group (now a part of Gartner), I participated in more than 1,400 teleconferences with clients and service providers and in my two years at Performance Monitor LLC, where I was chief intelligence officer, I conducted research into the field, covering SAP and Oracle systems integration, CRM systems integration, Application Development & Maintenance (the programming factories), and Application Outsourcing.

I think of it as six years of University of Enterprise Applications and a large segment of this research was devoted to SAP. I have recently left the research arena to get back into the world of SAP on a full-time basis and the revision of this book largely reflects the new insight I have gained through exposure to dozens of clients, a great variety of SAP systems integrators, other industry analysts, and a wealth of primary research.

In these six years, SAP has gone from being an 800 pound ERP gorilla to a supplier of a complete enterprise suite, including ERP, CRM, supply chain, and much more.

As of this writing, there is a high level of SAP maturity and while there is still a level of cautionary advice in the pages that follow, I am happy to be less shrill than in the past.

The table below summarizes some of the key changes between the 1993 to 2000 time period and present day (2007) that have been instrumental in reducing the risk, complexity, cost, and time to implement SAP software.

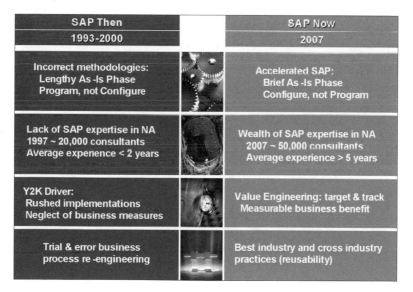

| SAP Then 1993-2000 | | SAP Now 2007 |
| --- | --- | --- |
| Incorrect methodologies: Lengthy As-Is Phase Program, not Configure | | Accelerated SAP: Brief As-Is Phase Configure, not Program |
| Lack of SAP expertise in NA 1997 ~ 20,000 consultants Average experience < 2 years | | Wealth of SAP expertise in NA 2007 ~ 50,000 consultants Average experience > 5 years |
| Y2K Driver: Rushed implementations Neglect of business measures | | Value Engineering: target & track Measurable business benefit |
| Trial & error business process re-engineering | | Best industry and cross industry practices (reusability) |

Implementation considerations have long varied depending upon the size of the client organization and in this edition I have added a new chapter: Yes, You Can: SAP for Small and Medium Enterprises.

In my years in the field, I have tended to show less interest in "how things work" than in "what they can do." This book will reflect this attitude and while much of the content covers the "how" of SAP implementations and deployment, readers should become highly aware of "what SAP can do" which is to enable horizontal workflow and organizational integration.

Throughout my twelve years in the world of SAP, I have had the good fortune to work with a great number of CEO's and have systematically asked them all of them at least this question: "Why did you go SAP?" Among the many responses I've had, the most succinct was that of a CEO in the oil industry back in 1997, who said, "Because now, when I put my foot on the gas, nothing happens." What he meant by that was that his current IT organization and systems were too complex, too highly interfaced, and too poorly integrated, with the result being that IT could not respond to business changes in reaction to threats or opportunities.

The central "why" of SAP is to enable your business to attain continuous and measurable business benefit.

As a prelude to Michael Connor's chapter, "Gaining Business Benefit with SAP," consider some examples of business benefit taken from the field.

| Retail & Distribution | |
|---|---|
| Key Performance Indicator | Impact |
| Inventory levels | - 30% |
| Warehouse space requirements | - 38% |
| Month-end financial closing process | - 5 days |
| Days sales outstanding (DSO) | - 44% |
| Staff devoted to receivables and collection | - 34% |
| Sourcing lead times | - 33% |
| Customer service, warehouse, and credit head count | 0% increase with >100% growth in sales |

| Manufacturing ||
|---|---|
| **Key Performance Indicator** | **Impact** |
| Factory schedule attainment | 10% |
| On-time shipping | 15% |
| Distribution productivity | + 15% in the shop<br>+ 20% in the office |
| Accounts receivable productivity | + 17% |
| Accounts payable productivity | + 16% |
| Purchasing productivity | + 36% |
| Output of air-handling equipment +18% without increasing the number of shop employees ||

| Consumer Bakery ||
|---|---|
| **Key Performance Indicator** | **Impact** |
| Order Fill Rate | *+ 2% pts |
| Returns | - 4% |
| Days in Inventory | -10% |
| Inventory Write-Downs | - 60% |
| Fixed-Asset Utilization | 5% pts |

This is the stuff of dreams for many CEOs who put their foot to the gas only to find that nothing happens.

SAP is not about information technology alone. It is about business solutions. Keep this in my mind as you read on.

...

For the past ten years I have offered a management seminar in SAP, targeted to middle management and up, which covers most of the subjects explored in this book. The original seminar lasted two days but few business people feel they can sacrifice that much time for a subject they think they could master in less. The seminar has since been recast for a single day and even that one day is often difficult for an executive to invest. I have been asked on more than one occasion to give a half-day seminar and once I was asked to scale down the seminar to one hour. In a nutshell.

This book is intended to provide that nutshell for those of you who desperately need to understand the business world of SAP but who do not have the time or inclination to attend a seminar. It is an objective view, drawn from direct experience, observation, and collaboration, and offers SAP from a business perspective, not a technical perspective. That is not to say that 'technology' will not make an appearance. One of the more heartfelt themes in what follows is that there is no longer a gulf between business and technology; further, the bridging of that gulf is why we have so many new subjects to master.

The subject of this book is business.

Herein is your nutshell.

CHAPTER 1

# How SAP Discovered the New World

# How SAP Discovered the New World

## A Quarter Century of Partial Victories

"Any sufficiently advanced technology is indistinguishable from magic," wrote Arthur C. Clarke in the early 1960's.

A stellar concept. But what if the word 'sufficiently' is removed? The magic vanishes.

Since the 1960's, twin notions have rested side by side: computer and nerd. The nerd with the pocket protector and a brace of colored pencils. The nerd with coke-bottle lens glasses held together at the bridge of the nose with scotch tape. The nerd who controls the programs that control the nervous system of the business. For over a quarter century, the nerd has been, if not your enemy, your *bête noire*, that pointy pebble in your business shoe, that reluctant, indecipherable human conduit between your information needs and your business satisfaction.

Through the years, the nerds have metamorphosed. Their languages have changed from Cobol and Fortran to RPG III and Basic and on to Java. Those coke bottle lenses are now contacts and the pocket protectors have long since been shed in favor of a light pen and the manly mouse. The nerds are no longer merely programmers or systems analysts, they are data base administrators, horizontal integration specialists, enterprise re-engineers, network administrators, or large stockholders in Microsoft or Google.

All the same, the notion persists that computers and the systems that run on them are the domain of nerds and that business people are still at their mercy. But it is not so.

A number of evolutionary breakthroughs, engineered by the nerds themselves, have contributed to a sea change in the way information systems are implemented, exploited, and maintained. Client/server technology, object-oriented programming, Internet and other telecom-related advances, as well as technologies that take advantage of all of these strides, have left us with a new business topography that is only recently coming clear to those of us in the business of information technology."

Key items on the new map include:

❑ A change in the role of business people vis-à-vis the information systems intended to support them.

❑ A corresponding power shift for the information systems people (the nerds in question).

❑ A radical shift in the life-cycle of information systems.

What has not changed, and what must change, is the attitude that most executives have in regard to information itself. Beyond the vision, the creation, and the implementation of information systems is the real nut of the deal: the use or abuse of information systems. Too many firms gather, store, and analyze information about them in a university-of-us fashion, with one study leading to another. For a business to be truly successful, and for that success to be maintained over time, information should be a catalyst for *informed* action.

## The Accelerating Failure of Traditional Information Systems

Misconceptions on the part of business people about the complexity of information systems and a parallel arrogance on the part of many systems people have led to a growing antagonism between these two groups. Whichever side you are coming from, you know the scenario.

❑ The business group, often represented by a steering committee, demands new services. The information systems group steps up to the plate and negotiations begin.

❑ The business group's ability to define the needed services is limited to a business point of view, but the information systems people are asking detailed questions (field lengths, sort orders, interfacing rules, procedural rules). The business people seldom have the time or knowledge to adequately answer all of these questions. The information systems people have to make decisions in their stead.

❑ Functional specifications are approved by the business group and turned over to the 'techies' for a round of technical specifications, programming, and testing.

❑ Direct users are trained. Data are loaded to the new system or converted from existing systems.

❑ In the interim, months have passed, business light years. The newly installed system is geared to win last year's war and the business people are already asking for changes. Systems people argue that they have delivered what business asked for. The cycle of antagonism and disappointment continues.

This same cycle has visibly accelerated over the past ten years, during which time business has grown more and more complex. The frustrations of both business people (demand) and systems people (supply) have grown accordingly. At lunchtime, a sales director reads an article in a biz journal about gee-whiz new technology and how it is going to change the face of sales and then returns to his desk to mull over a month-old printout of 'hot' prospects. A committee of directors puts the seal of approval on a restructuring plan that will save their firm millions over the first six months only to find that the systems needed to support the restructuring may take twelve months to build and implement.

"When I put my foot on the gas, nothing happens," complains an oil refinery CEO. Hundreds of thousands of executives have shared this thought over the past quarter century. Companies have often been doomed to move according to the speed of their information systems, a relative snail's pace when a simple jog would yield a fortune.

Partial victories have come every two to four years. Consider the following technological leaps and how the success promised by each has been compromised:

**The stand-alone desktop computer** became commonplace in the mid-1980's and promised vast economies in the financial and administrative arena and a dispersal of data centers from the data processing departments to individual users. The economies have been realized, as has a certain democratization of information, but there has been another edge to this very sharp sword: the cacophony of data that emanates from "personal" computers. We see renegade profit & loss analyses unscroll from printers on shop floors, sixteen-color bar charts generated by accounting staff that "prove" the need to eliminate product lines, and enough 9 point spreadsheets with decimals and percentages to wallpaper the Grand Canyon. My computer says, oh yeah, well *my* computer says...

**The PC network,** which quickly followed the rise of the stand-alone desktop, was accompanied by bold predictions of 'paperless companies,' in which the volume of business data would expand but the paper needed to carry it would contract (much in the same way credit cards 'expanded' purchasing power while diminishing the need for wrinkled dollar bills.) While it is true that PC networks eliminate much of the data redundancy that once existed – and have clearly served us well in the realm of data sharing and transmission – it is equally true that companies like International Paper and Georgia Pacific are doing more business than ever in 8 1/2 x 11 paper products.

(In the same fashion, we find that the Internet has not, and will not replace our love of newsprint and the feel of a paperback in our hands. We will not wean ourselves from *hard* copy all too soon.)

**PC Mainframe connections** promised a consistency of data in which PC users or user groups could tap into the mainframe well for raw enterprise data and analyze them with powerful PC tools. But these connections have only led to an acceleration of data 'noise' rather than information, and the claim that the raw data come from 'the computer' has been compromised by the manipulation of those data with the PC.

**The dispersion of data entry** from centralized "keypunch" to source entry, whether via keyboard, barcode reader, or scanner has fulfilled the promise of vastly improved data integrity and rapid data capture. The other side of this shiny coin has been the emerging need to train systems users to ever more sophisticated functions. The failure here has not been technological and cannot be pinned on the nerds; it is the failure of business (read=management) to sufficiently grasp the need for education. The notion of user training as the key to success with new systems has long since been surpassed by the reality of systems use: education at various levels is a necessity to which most firms only give lip service.

**The shift from centralized (mainframe) to distributive processing** (smaller computers in a network) has delivered faster local turnaround for data and allowed for applications that better fit user group needs. Specific software has been acquired and often customized for specific needs. However, distributive processing has also led to a massive multiplication of interfaces, not only site-to-site interfaces, but also between software packages of disparate origin.

One highly visible failure of distributive processing, as opposed to centralized, has been the decay of corporate-level management information. The timeliness of data collection is always questionable and the accuracy of the data suspect. This failure can be squarely pinned on the insoluble and costly burden of interfacing.

**The ascendance of the CIO** during the 1980's signaled a welcome departure from a hierarchical structure in which information systems were the domain of finance people. For the first time, companies stopped looking at 'data processing' as an overhead and began to see it as a reducer of overhead. However, once freed from the shackles of finance, information specialists discovered the dark side of their new autonomy: ceaseless, unanswerable demand by business people for better business systems.

By the early 1990's, we had arrived at what constituted an information stalemate. In sum, our distributed systems were unmanageable, our data unreliable, and our systems staff increasingly unable to deliver new systems supports in a timely fashion. And then along came SAP.

## Computerize This

CEOs do not spend much of their time thinking about computer technology. Their muse time tends to embrace competitive analyses, potential acquisitions, corporate restructuring, and the fluctuating value of their stock options.

Senior executives are on pretty much the same paper cloud, although their focus will naturally descend to their patch of turf, a corporate division, a product line, a geographic sector, or whatever. Few are interested in the day-to-operations of a company and if you review the last half dozen projects your company has undertaken, you will probably find that they were instigated by employees below the senior management borderline.

All the same, the systems you have today reflect past management decisions and the systems you have tomorrow will reflect today's management decisions.

There may be a coterie amongst you that believes that SAP is the wide doorway through which your firm can enter a more productive and profitable future. Without the consent and understanding of senior management, that door will never be cracked open.

By the same token, "computerize this" has too often been a management order in firms that are failing. Computerization will not help half as much as a change in business processes. In fact, computerization alone can be disastrous. A company that is losing money with slow and inefficient data systems can accelerate its losses with fast and efficient data systems.

## How SAP Discovered the New World

I never thought I would see myself as any kind of a pioneer, but in the realm of micro-computing, I have to admit that I go way back, all the way to 1980, the year I first touched a TRS 80 and blinked some Basic code across a hazy green screen. Shortly thereafter, I was introduced to the miracle of VisiCalc (the Adam of spreadsheets) and I used a Commodore Pet that possessed all of 64K of memory. Once VisiCalc was loaded, I was left with 12K and a little memory counter in the lower left of the screen that would deflate to 8K or 6K once I keyed in an "exotic" formula like @Sum (A1..A14).

What makes me feel like a pioneer is the relative power, and cost, of micro-computing nowadays. (I used the word 'nowadays.' Isn't that a pioneer-style word?) I no longer have a memory counter to deal with and 64K is chump change in a world now measured in terabytes. The laptop, which is mother to this book, has a gazillion megabytes of memory and I have made a three-dimensional spreadsheet that offers every possible imagined statistic for my fantasy baseball team, yet I still have miles of memory available.

|  |  | Memory | Storage | Applications | 1997 $ |
|------|----------------|--------|---------|--------------------------|---------|
| 1980 | TRS 80 | 64K | 256K | Basic | $3000 |
| 1982 | Commodore Pet | 128K | 256K | Visicalc | $4000 |
| 1985 | IBM PC XT | 512K | 10 MB | Lotus, Wordperfect | $4000 |
| 1989 | Victor Luggable | 1 MB | 400 MB | Lotus, WP, DB4 | $4000 |
| 1995 | Dell Portable | 16 MB | 1 GB | Lotus, WP, DB4, Internet | $4000 |
| 1997 | Gateway Laptop | 48 MB | 2 GB | MS Office | $4500 |
| 2005 | Dell Latitude | 512 MB | 74 GB | The works | $1400 |

*The authors's micro-computer genealogy*

My status as pioneer is only as a business user. More clever technical folks were fiddling with gizmo computers since well before 1980. In the spring of 1973, design work was completed on the Micral, the first non-kit computer based on a microprocessor (the Intel 8008). Built in France, the Micral was advertised in the U.S., but was not successful there. The term "micro-computer" is often attributed to the apparition of the Micral, but may well have resulted from the fact that during this same period there was a major distinction between mainframe systems and minis (this being the period of time in which distributive processing was all the rage), so these little tykes had to be referred to as microcomputers. In the interim, we have progressed from desktops to luggables to laptops to palmtops but this evolution has not yet led us to develop the pin-like fingers necessary for some of the keyboards included with these itsy-bitsy computers.

In past decades, storage space and memory had to be carefully managed and cutting corners with record sizes was a part of every analyst's daily life. One result of space management was the Year 2000 debacle that so many companies faced. The savings of those two digits "19" before each year entry may not now seem to be of any import, but before client/server technology came along (as well as the evolution of storage media) two digits per record times 100,000 records was 200K of saved space! That 200K is now a whiff of air, but twenty years ago, the term gigabyte only applied to supercomputers and floppy diskettes were just coming onto the scene.

At any rate, the processing power of all computers has taken generational leaps just about every two years since 1980. In this same timeframe, connectivity between microcomputers and mainframes has also had a rapid evolution.

> SAP has become the Columbus of the information systems world. The company sailed west with the powers of micro-computing and east with the complete and integrated applications suite and met at a median point we know as client/server technology.

In the mid 1980's, data could be directly downloaded from mainframes to PCs. This major step was followed by transactional connectivity and, by the early 1990's, to client/server technology. These days, mainframes and desktops can be configured so that applications, data, and presentation servers can be tuned to company traffic and needs. Scalability is accordion-like as processing power can be moved from the mainframe to individual desktops or separate networks and back again.

In terms of applications software, there has not been an evolution to parallel that of processing power. Various software suppliers have tended to churn out packages that have been limited to single platforms (HP or Sun or IBM), thus requiring prospective clients to have the platform in question if they want to use the software. During these same years, distributive processing was the norm, in which individual company sites had their own hardware and software and data consolidations were made via interfaces.

As a result, companies today have a variety of platforms and operating systems, a variety of applications written in various languages, and a tangled web of interfaces holding it all together (or not).

Slowly, and at first quietly, SAP AG built something different. Four engineers broke away from IBM Germany and began peddling a mainframe financial package in 1972. In 1976, they tacked on a materials management module that was integrated with the financials. There followed a sales and distribution module, then production planning, and inevitably more and more application modules. Each succeeding module remained fully integrated with the others and the understandable popularity of this horizontal integration led to the rise of SAP AG throughout Europe, South Africa, and Australia.

The two evolutionary curves that were most prominent in the mid-1980's were the power of micro-computing and the crying need for applications that could be integrated without the complications and costs of interfacing.

SAP AG took note of these two evolutionary curves and, with the announcement of R/3 in late 1992, it has become the Columbus of the information systems world. Banking on the then revolutionary premise that business processes are not vertical but are flat (horizontal), the company sailed west with the powers of micro-computing and east with the complete and integrated applications suite that could replace the failing vertically integrated and interfaced applications of yore.

## How SAP Rose to the Top

Brilliance, innovation, and daring are seldom sufficient for the launching of a business phenomenon. Luck (otherwise known as the confluence of events) played a major role in the early stratospheric climb of R/3 licensing. In 1993, just as R/3 was gaining a foothold in North America, Michael Hammer and James Champy published "Re-engineering the Corporation, A Manifesto for Business Revolution." Over the next year and a half, more than 1.7 million copies of this book were sold, with nearly half of this total attributed to North America. In brief, Hammer and Champy describe the need for businesses to radically re-invent themselves in order to bring about dramatic improvements in performance. The accent is on the word *radical.* They compare reorganizations and structural tinkering to "rearranging the deck chairs on the Titanic" and seek to demonstrate that business processes rather than organizational structures are the subject at hand.

The simplicity and brilliance of this message are confounded by the fact that it is still very hard to reinvent an existing company. Company traditions and culture, executive turf protection, conflicting strategies, and natural corporate inertia all tend to resist radical re-engineering. Further, information systems have to be radically recast to support full-scale re-engineering, a message that is ignored in the Hammer and Champy opus. This is where the announcement of R/3 could not have come at a better time. CEOs leaped at R/3 as a means to the promised land of what is now commonly referred to as BPR..

SAP marketing followed this trend to the letter as sales efforts have targeted senior management rather than information systems management; that is to say, SAP sells its software as a business solution, not a technology solution.

The announcement of SAP R/3 with client/server and workflow coincided with the vast wave of "downsizing" that began in the late 1980's. As unimaginative as downsizing can be, it leaves in its wake a need for the survivors to re-invent how their company will continue to function. It is, according to the Hammer and Champy vision, sufficiently radical. It should not be surprising to realize that, in 1993 and 1994, SAP R/3 was seen as a CEO's 'downsizing partner.' In reality, SAP's product is no such thing, but the perception did no harm whatever to sales.

More cogent to the success of SAP are 1) the high quality and flexibility of its product, 2) a rigid devotion to research and development, and 3) its strategic partnerships with platform vendors, consulting firms, and competitors.

SAP has long since moved beyond R/3 into mySAP ERP and, more recently, into NetWeaver. This book is not about the technology of SAP and although the distinctions between R/3, mySAP, and NetWeaver are of major import, they will only matter after a reader has absorbed the basics that are in this book.

As such, we will be referring quite simply to SAP software with an accent on the more contemporary SAP/NetWeaver world.

## SAP in Leaps and Bounds

In 1992, just before R/3 was announced, SAP America's revenues were $1 80M. Final 1998 revenues approached $2B. As of August 2007, SAP claims roughly 40,000 customers and 2006 global revenues approached $13 billion. In short, growth has been rampant and generally unchecked for close to fifteen years.

Until 1992, when R/3 was introduced, the great majority of SAP licenses were in Europe, with a smattering of others in Australia, South Africa, and North America. Since that time, as SAP support for both R/3 and English has improved, North America has come to represent the most important part of SAP revenues.

Through the years, SAP revenue has shifted from a high percentage of new licenses to roughly one third new licensing, one third maintenance, and one third consulting and support. The migration from client-server-based R/3 toward web-based services and NetWeaver is in recognition of the evolution of platforms and architectures beyond client server and NetWeaver has spurred new license sales

R/3 thrust SAP into an international limelight. It should be noted that some of the fuel to this fire was the Y2K crisis. Companies facing the need to correct existing software found it preferable to throw out old systems and SAP was a popular new choice. As the millennium approached, new licensing flattened out and the curve remained flat in 2000. Software revenues dropped in 2002 and 2003 but have since rebounded as SAP has continued to offer evolutions of its own self (new functionality, new features) as well as a Customer Relationship Management offering, supply chain (APO), and the new NetWeaver technology.

In this same time period, SAP expertise has grown dramatically as both clients and SAP consulting firms have increased knowledge of how to implement and use the software. Thus, SAP has moved into a mature third phase of its existence that has resulted in solid growth.

CHAPTER 2

# What is SAP?

- ❏ The Shelf Life of This Chapter is Questionable
- ❏ Coping with the SAP Alphabet
- ❏ Features of SAP
- ❏ Core Business Applications of SAP
- ❏ Workflow Applications
- ❏ Accelerated Solutions with NetWeaver
- ❏ And All the Rest
- ❏ Critical Distinctions Between SAP and What You Know

# What is SAP?

## The Shelf Life of This Chapter is Questionable

As any good SAP-watcher knows, no moss grows under those munchkin feet in Walldorf, Germany and Palo Alto, California where SAP R&D takes place. Even as I type this paragraph at 120 wpm, ABAP/4 code is coursing through SAP pipelines and wrapping itself into beta releases and SAP Dot Com announcements. No book could keep up with a thousand bit-byte ABAP/4 zombies, and this book will not try. Even as this book goes to print, new SAP releases will render any description of the product somewhat dated.

This first section covers some of the basics of SAP, the company, and its array of products.

If you already are familiar with the basics, skip to the next section.

## Coping with the SAP Alphabet

Within the world of SAP, there are many variations on the meaning of the letters S A P.

To the paranoid, it is a German code for "Thanks for the Euros." To a careless reader, it is Spa misspelled. To a disgruntled customer, Shut up And Pay. To a concerned project manager, Say A Prayer. To the competition, Sulk And Pout. To an SAP consultant, Suitcase And Passport.

Ess Ay Pee is how it is pronounced, not sap as in rap, cap, or slap. Your computers aren't ibem, they are IBM. Eds are not Edwards when you are talking about EDS. Anyway, all SAP means is Systems, Applications, and Products (loose translation).

SAP AG, headquartered in Walldorf, Germany, is the supplier. The core ERP product we will be referring to through the remainder of this book is collective (R/3, mySAP, NetWeaver). If you are at a point at which those distinctions matter, there are parts of this book you may wish to pass by.

Just to be clear, the world at large still refers to both the company *and* the product as SAP, as in "We decided to implement SAP because of its integrated data base."

Beyond these distinctions, there is a vast world of initial-speak in the world of SAP, beginning with the applications. Financials are referred to as Eff Eye, Sales & Distribution as Ess Dee, and Materials Management as Em Em.

As a basic sampling:

| Initial | Meaning |
|---------|---------|
| FI | Financials |
| SD | Sales & Distribution |
| MM | Materials Management |
| PP | Production Planning |
| HR | Human Resources |

As will be seen (to the point of distraction) the applications are tightly integrated and so initials are often glued together to better define terms. Someone working in the Process Industry version of Production Planning will be referred to as a PP-PI. If you see SD-MM, you will understand that it refers the elements of Materials Management that are integrated with Sales & Distribution.

If you are an apprentice to SAP, there is no need to learn all of the initial-speak. Through the remainder of this publication, we will make every effort to spell things out.

## Features of SAP

The allure of SAP software is not found in its business modules alone, but in its overall features. Functional comparisons of SAP to its smaller competitors often lead to misconceptions because an apples-to-apples comparison of applications fails to take into account the enterprise-wide nature of SAP. Indeed, it is often said that competitors' packages for individual applications stack up nicely against SAP but, as discussed in Chapter 1, individual applications are less and less cogent to business as we know it.

In this section, we explore the operational and business features of SAP that have contributed to its phenomenal success and its status as the least understood business product of its generation.

These features are:

❑ Complete Suite of Integrated Applications

❑ Open Systems Architecture

❑ Global Business Architecture

❑ Transparency Between SAP and PC Applications

❑ Audit Trail and Data Integrity Controls

### Complete Suite of Integrated Applications

This is by far the most alluring and powerful feature of SAP software and hinges on two operative elements: complete and integrated.

Numerous competitors offer integrated applications, but none compares to the vastness of SAP's list of business applications. Beyond core business functions (Finance, Sales & Distribution, Materials Management, etc.), SAP includes Plant Maintenance,

Quality Management, Project System, Human Resources, Production Planning, and much, much more. Further, there are industry-specific solutions for oil and gas, chemicals, retail, and a host of other industries. SAP tries very hard to be all things to all companies, and although it fails to supply everything under the sun, there has been a continual flow of new applications, upgrades, and industry-specific bolt-ons.

What is fairly magical, however, is that all of these applications still work with a single, integrated data base. The significance of this feature cannot be understated.

- Data integrity is assured.

- Data handling and maintenance are vastly simplified.

- No interfaces are required between applications.

- Transactions are updated across the board on an immediate basis. Thus, management information is up-to-the-minute, not as of the last batch run.

SAP is not alone in providing real-time data updates, but it does stand alone in providing real time updating in an integrated fashion throughout a complete applications suite.

When a wing nut drops on a production line, SAP hears a ping in accounting, materials management, and possibly one or two other applications.

## Open Systems Architecture

Since the beginning of cyber time, applications have been written according to the house rules as laid down by the platform on which the software will run. Each hardware vendor used to offer a different operating system that worked with different programming languages. A company with IBM hardware that wanted to purchase software that only ran on Hewlett Packard platforms was out of luck. Other software firms have closed the gap in this regard, but SAP was the first to provide truly open system architecture and this fact alone fueled sales way back in the mid-1990's.

Large firms that have distributed their processing across disparate sites have by and large developed heterogeneous computer parks, mixing IBM with HP or Dell with NEC.

SAP eliminates the platform question with an open systems architecture, which functions on a number of different platforms. These include HP, IBM, Sun, and various others. Further, clients have a choice of data base systems and operating systems.

The immediate phenomenal success of R/3 would have been seriously compromised if the software had not been built in such a way. Acquiring and implementing SAP software is costly enough; if clients are also required to change over entire computer parks, the pill may be too large to swallow.

The 'portability' of SAP software will also have an effect on the life cycle of your system. As your company expands or contracts, the hardware base will expand or contract, but you will be able to jiggle SAP into any size environment without having to give it a makeover. In similar fashion, if your company expands through acquisition and the acquired firm has different hardware, SAP can probably fold it into your organization without major new hardware expense.

### Global Business Architecture

Facture, factura, rechnung, invoice. These are all the same to SAP. Though Made In Germany, the software is now fully global and is the only applications suite on the market that can make this claim.

Its global features include:

*Screens and Language*

The language appearing on screens, on-line help, and on-line documentation can appear in whatever language the user's log-on dictates. Obviously, not *all* languages in the universe are available. You can have English, French, German, Swedish. You cannot have Urdu, not yet. You can have Japanese, Italian, Spanish, Arabic, Dutch, Greek, and Texan. You cannot have Latin, but you can see roman numerals on occasion.

As of this writing, SAP software is said to be available in more than thirty languages.

The fact that language is user-driven means that users in various countries can all be logged on at the same time, each working in their local language, using whatever parts of the system they desire. As an old story goes, an order can be entered in German in Hamburg, the materials can be ordered from Paris in French for delivery in Dutch to Brussels for manufacturing, and invoiced in English to the customer in Des Moines.

*Multi-Currency*

Beyond language, country-specific considerations are taken into account by SAP. Multiple currencies can be handled in a variety of ways (fixed rates, rates updated via external data base, average periodic rates, et al). Further, tax considerations by jurisdiction (country, province, state, NAFTA, GATT, EC) are addressed as table-driven system controls.

## Transparency Between SAP Applications and PC Applications

Microsoft and SAP have long been engaged in a fairly serious partnership and as the Windows standard for graphical user interface has come to dominate the world, SAP offers exceptional integration between Microsoft applications and its own applications. With the flexibility afforded by multi-tier client service, Microsoft (or other PC-based) applications can be run separately or within the context of SAP.

For example, data can be extracted with standard SAP tools and manipulated with Microsoft Excel, Word, Access, or whatever. If your firm has a Microsoft background and users are already familiar with Windows navigation and standards, SAP software will not look all that foreign to them.

This Microsoft/SAP transparency has recently been upgraded with the 2007 announcement of Duet, which provides great synchronization between Outlook, Microsoft Exchange, and SAP processes.

### Audit Trail and Data Integrity Controls

SAP software is an auditor's dream. Every transaction is logged and 'fingerprinted' as to who made the transaction (user ID), when it was made, and what it was. Further, there is no way to simply void or delete errors. Mistaken input has to be backed out of the system and error checking can include the matching of transactions that lead to an error and its subsequent resolution.

The system disciplines are rigid, which often leads people to complain about how inflexible the system can be. Sometimes this argument comes from the same people who seldom follow an agenda during meetings, push on doors marked 'pull,' and never order what's on the menu.

## Core Business Applications of SAP

We will first zoom in on the hardy perennials, the absolute core of the applications suite, and then some of the other key applications (referred to herein as Workflow applications) and focus solely on the characteristics and features important to management.

The core business applications offered by SAP are the same as those offered (individually, in most cases) by traditional package software vendors: Finance, Controlling, Sales & Distribution, Materials Management, Production Planning, and Human Resources. SAP Financials have had a solid reputation of being at the top of the charts in the world of software, most often cited as the equal of any stand-alone financials package you can find. The Sales & Distribution module was criticized by some in years past as "heavy" and difficult to master. This is because SAP is one product intended to serve diverse masters. Sales and distribution varies widely between retail, build-to-order, manufacturing, health, banking, and other industries. Such diversity has its natural consequences to Materials Management and Production Planning (PP) as industry-specific considerations require SAP to dance with several feet at once. When you seek implementation, there is at

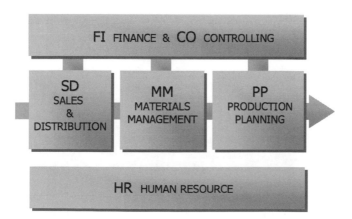

first a tangle of sorts that SAP unravels, with increasing success, through its industry-specific templates and aids.

Few companies implement much more than these core applications first. Most begin with FI and then carry on. Others implement all of these core applications in one go. Still other companies implement *some* of these core applications and *interface* them to legacy systems; this does not always make good sense but adds a mountain of consulting hours and keeps people busy.

## Workflow Applications

Plant Maintenance, Project Systems, Workflow, and Quality Maintenance represent a second tier of SAP modules. Whereas Plant Maintenance is more of a functional application, the others relate directly to the flow of work throughout an enterprise. Plant Maintenance and Quality Maintenance are just what they are named. Each has industry-specific wrinkles and are tightly integrated with Production Planning and, to some degree, with Materials Management.

The Workflow module allows for an automation of business processes, combining human and computer 'events' or activities that trigger one another to the conclusion of a process. After basic business process re-engineering (that box-arrow-box exercise), the system can be configured to address horizontal business flow. However, Workflow takes this a step further by automating the process. Each event or activity is assigned to a person or the system, its duration is fixed, and work that is relative to a defined process is routed throughout an organization.

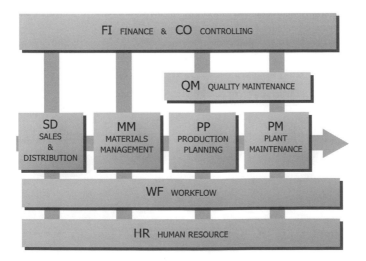

In the preceding pages, we have described primarily the Enterprise Resource Planning (ERP) modules but SAP's offering spans much wider than ERP. Here is the full menu:

SAP Business Suite
    SAP Customer Relationship Management
    SAP ERP
    SAP Product Lifecycle Management
    SAP Supply Chain Management
SAP Supplier Relationship Management
SAP Manufacturing
SAP Service and Asset Management
SAP xApps Composite Applications
    SAP xApp Analytic
    SAP xApps for Mobile Business
Duet

## Accelerated Solutions with NetWeaver

SAP has invested heavily since 2003 in the development of NetWeaver which is the foundation for Enterprise Services Architecture, or ESA. This architecture offers increased levels of adaptability, flexibility, and openness. "Openness" means that SAP applications can work with non-SAP applications. Such openness is one of the key distinctions between SAP and the various components of the Oracle offering. While Oracle wants its clients to have nothing but Oracle software under the hood, SAP recognizes that most organizations will necessarily have other applications software and therefore need an architecture that will enable complete integration in terms of application processing, business intelligence, and data integrity and harmonization.

Some of the key components of NetWeaver are as follows:

**SAP Enterprise Portal** provides a complete portal infrastructure along with knowledge management and collaboration software. An enterprise portal gives end users access to multiple types of information and applications through a standard interface.

**SAP Business Intelligence** makes information actionable by helping companies identify, integrate, and analyze disparate business data from both SAP and non-SAP sources.

**SAP Master Data Management** is the foundation for providing harmonized, consistent information to both SAP and non-SAP applications across the enterprise.

**SAP Exchange Infrastructure** provides open integration technologies that support process-centric collaboration among SAP and non-SAP components both within and beyond enterprise boundaries.

**SAP Web Application Server** is a development and deployment platform that supports Web services, business applications, and standards-based development based on key technologies such as J2EE and ABAP™.

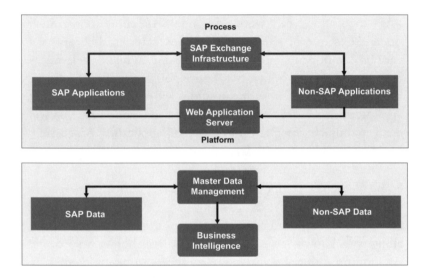

## And All the Rest

Having offered a cursory overview of the company and the features and applications of SAP, we cannot state that we have told you what SAP is. In both breadth of scope and depth of functionality, the software is seemingly boundless and SAP itself offers fat 9-inch-by-12-inch color-coded volumes for each of the applications.

We have not yet mentioned Assets Management, Inventory Management, Warehouse Management, or Service Management. Beyond these subjects, there are report and query aids, SAPScript, Data Warehousing, and more. But this is a concise business guide, not an exhaustive technical text, so let us simply carry on in that vein, confident that the SAP pool is far deeper than this chapter cares to say.

Further, SAP has extended its product well beyond the realm of pure ERP (as described thus far). There is a robust Customer Relationship Management suite as well as supply chain (APO), advanced portals capability that allows for the commingling of various software on a single user's screen, advanced web middleware, and much more. This book is not intended to cover the entire SAP product galaxy and should remain only a point of entry into the subject. For more details on the full gamut of SAP product, browse with confidence through www.sap.com.

## Critical Distinctions Between SAP and What You Know

When in the field, consultants tend to repeat certain phrases over and over. Often, these repetitions include sighs of exasperation, but the phrases must be repeated time and again because of the distinctions between SAP and what you have known in the past.

Among these phrases are:

"SAP is a business project, not an IT project"

"We're not programming here, we're configuring"

"It is integrated software, so what you do in (fill in department name) will immediately affect (fill in department name)"

Often, the difficulty in getting key messages across lies in the experience of the audience. Nearly everyone involved in an SAP implementation has already participated in at least one traditional IT project and will tend to rely upon that experience as instructive. It may well be, but only partially so.

Do not entrench yourself into a Maginot Line of past experience and how you won the last war. In order to accelerate a conversion to SAP thinking, you should absorb and retain the lessons of this chapter, which will take a great strain off both yourselves and your consultants.

### Critical Distinction #1:
*SAP is a Business Endeavor, Not a Computer Endeavor*

As elaborated in the first chapter, business folks are no longer the hostages of computer technology. In this light, there are multiple distinctions between SAP and what you know.

The first is that business people, not information technology people, directly determine what the systems should do. Further, business people also bend existing software to their wills. This is done by configuring SAP software according to established rules and methods.

The distinction between programming and configuring is of huge import. Programming requires 'technical' knowledge. Configuring requires 'business' knowledge.

Configuring is the setting of business tables that determine the format, the nature, the location, and the destination of information.

Programming is the creation of codes that manipulate the format, the nature, the location, and the destination of information.

On the previous page there is a sample configuration table. Such a table is simpler for a business person to understand than is a series of Java programs.

In essence, SAP software is comprised of hundreds of tables like this one, all of which drive data according to the rules laid down by business people.

This leads to a second sub-distinction, which is the disappearance of the traditional negotiation between business and IT groups for new information services or changes to existing services. In sum, SAP provides business software for business people, created by business people, and maintained by business people as business evolves.

### Critical Distinction #2 :
*Integration = Enterprise-wide = Horizontal Processes*

Your project will not succeed if you think of separately building individual applications in the way you have in the past. Decisions that you make about Materials Management will certainly have repercussions in Sales & Distribution and Financials, and possibly in Production Planning.

Further, your core implementation will take you longer than would the implementation of a new accounting package or a customized sales order processing module. Remember, you are not simply installing software, you are re-inventing the manner in which your company functions. Thus, your implementation team will be comprised of representatives from throughout the company and each will be tempted to defend the turf of his or her current domain. Turf protection is harmful to enterprise-wide thinking.

Another factor of an enterprise-wide undertaking is *the heightening of risk*. The stakes are higher, the potential benefits more dramatic, and the costs more visible than for a traditional systems undertaking. A lot of nervous activity occurs in such an environment. Emotions are jangled and tempers are tested. This is why change management is a subset of SAP projects. (More on this to come.)

### Critical Distinction #3:
*Integration Places an Added Burden on Direct Users*

One of the prime sources of resistance to an SAP implementation is the direct (or end) user group. This resistance is often related to a simple fear of change or a loathing to learn another system. This much can be overcome with good project leadership, but another cause for resistance to SAP is the added burden that it places on such users. This burden takes two forms:

**Time:** Compared to most legacy systems, SAP software requires more input and more complex input for the majority of its functions. Users will rightfully complain that for SAP software they are forced to use three screens to fulfill a function that required only a single screen for legacy systems.

**Authority/Responsibility:** Workflow eliminates a major portion of supervisory tasks and the integrated nature of SAP software puts power into the hands of the users. The entry of data is no longer simply a chore of reporting to the system but is now an instigator of action. Someone entering even supplementary data to an existing sales order is virtually working for accounting (cash flow), materials management (requisition), and production planning (for manufacturing and delivery dates) all at the same time. Sniff the air and it smells of empowerment; not that Dilbertville bogus empowerment, but the real thing.

**Critical Distinction #4:**
*The System Lifecycle is Vastly Extended*

No longer will you have to envision replacing your software wholesale or in large segments every five years or so. As configurable software, your SAP software should be modified according to changes in business climate and your firm's ambitions. Since these changes should not require re-programming (or, worse, maintenance of interfaces), system degradation should not occur.

Further, you should be anticipating a new post-implementation organization in which your SAP-savvy staff remains a team that can drive continual business improvement while your IT group takes on a technical support role.

CHAPTER 3

# SAP by the Numbers
*by Paul Reynolds*

❏ Follow the Numbers

❏ Start at the Beginning

❏ Get it Done

❏ Common Pitfalls of SAP Projects

❏ Goals and the Problems that Hinder Them

❏ Small and Mid-Market SAP Considerations

# SAP by the Numbers

## Follow the Numbers

By the title of this chapter you might be expecting to read about financial TLA's (three letter acronyms) like TCO, ROI, and impact on EPS. The chapter title is actually a double entendre that doesn't have anything to do with financial metrics.

You can observe a lot
just by watching.
Yogi Berra

The purpose of this chapter is to share the collective wisdom of 301 organizations that completed their SAP implementation in 2006. Their participation in a landmark SAP research study reveals several key findings that can benefit organizations about to embark on their own journey.

So, the story that is about to unfold is credible because of the sheer volume of study participants (power in numbers) and we will use their experiences as our guide (follow the numbers).

To set the stage, a major research study was undertaken to gain insight into various aspects of SAP projects. The focus of the research was not about the software, but about the services associated with the implementation. After reaching out to more than 500,000 IT and business people, the experiences of 809 SAP projects were assembled into a common framework. The findings presented here are based on the most recent 301 SAP systems integration projects studied.

Undoubtedly, as you embark upon your own journey you will talk to a handful of reference clients of each of the leading SAP consultancies (aka systems integrators). The findings that follow are a composite of 301 reference clients who have shared their stories about why they chose they integrator, the types of problems they experienced along the way, and how effectively their goals were attained.

By following the numbers we can watch how their mindset shifts as they move from the buying process to the implementation process. Further, the numbers will reveal how different types of problems impact goal attainment. Your organization can benefit by avoiding some of the pitfalls that others have fallen into when traveling the same road.

## Start at the Beginning

Once your organization has committed to SAP, the next step is finding an integration partner to not only implement the software but also to adhere to your vision. Of the 301 clients we interviewed, 233 were involved in the selection decision for their systems integrator.

Because SAP implementations are so broad, there are a lot of things buyers must consider when selecting a systems integrator. In an effort to learn what separates one prospective firm from another, study participants identified as many as three reasons why they chose their integrator over the others on the shortlist.

The table on the following page shows the eighteen reasons that were tested. The reasons span a variety of topics, including financial considerations, core corporate capabilities, branding elements, the delivery team, end user training, and post-implementation planning.

When clients hire an SAP systems integrator, they are hiring the firm and their people. The core capabilities of the firm will remain over time – things like their methodologies, tools, partner networks, etc. The people, however, will change, as promotions, job changes, and retirements inevitably happen. Therefore, clients should place a strong emphasis on the systems integrators' methodologies and tools during the selection process. These results reveal that clients do just that as methodologies and tools is most frequently cited as the reason one firm was chosen over another.

People skills, however, are more difficult to assess. The second and third most frequently cited differentiators are people-related: prior experience with vendor and provider reputation. Unfortunately, neither of these is a true assessment of their capabilities – they are impressions of what it is like to work a consultancy.

Superior personnel, technical capabilities, and vertical industry experience are better measures of skills (though more difficult to assess). Technical capabilities is fourth on the list, which is good. Superior personnel and vertical industry experience drop to the middle of the list, however.

| Reasons Clients Chose Their SAP Systems Integrator Over Others on their Shortlist | |
| --- | --- |
| Number of Projects | 233 |
| Strong methodology and tools | 25% |
| Prior direct experience with vendor | 24% |
| Provider reputation | 21% |
| Technical advantage/capabilities | 20% |
| Strong partner network | 19% |
| Price (eg. rates, overall cost) | 19% |
| Promised timely delivery | 19% |
| Superior personnel/expertise | 18% |
| Knowledge transfer capabilities | 15% |
| Vertical industry experience | 13% |
| Performance measurement capabilities | 13% |
| Span/flexibility of services | 12% |
| Compelling delivery model | 12% |
| Contract terms (eg. terms, SLA's) | 11% |
| Superior customer references | 11% |
| Compelling road map to fulfill vision | 9% |
| Over-riding personal relationship/deal making | 8% |
| Thrive after go-live strategy | 3% |

*Respondents could choose up to 3 differentiators.*
*Percentages will not sum to 100%*
*Table based on those involved in the SI selection decision*
*Copyright 2007 Performance Monitor LLC*

At the outset of this chapter I told you this chapter wasn't about financials. SAP buying teams can't get the financials out of their heads, however, as price has a significant influence over one in five selection decisions.

Note some of the items that are towards the bottom of this list, considerations such as "thrive after Go-Live strategy," "compelling delivery model," and "span/flexibility of services." Perhaps clients feel these are "table stakes" and that those on the shortlist have already demonstrated how their project will be delivered and that their world will be better when the project is complete.

## Get It Done

After the selection process is complete the focus changes to delivery. Timely delivery (defined as "delivered the project on or ahead of schedule"), staff experience (defined as "leveraged strong ERP skills"), and staff quality (defined as "leveraged strong consulting skills") are understandably at the top of the list – "we're on the clock, let's get it done."

| Importance of Criteria Upon Project Start | |
|---|---|
| Overall | 301 |
| Timely Delivery | 11.8 |
| Staff Experience | 11.6 |
| Staff Quality | 10.5 |
| Methodology & Tools | 9.7 |
| Knowledge Transfer | 9.2 |
| Delivery Model | 7.4 |
| Adherence to Vision | 7.3 |
| Industry Focus | 7.2 |
| Post-Implementation Planning | 6.8 |
| Measurement | 6.7 |
| Agility | 6.1 |
| Partner Network | 5.6 |
| *Respondents allocated 100 points across criteria* | |
| *Copyright 2007 Performance Monitor LLC* | |

Actually, each of the top six elements on this table has a strong "get it done" focus. Methodology and tools is listed fourth, which places strong emphasis on the process. Knowledge Transfer ranks fifth, respectively, and shows a commitment for the organization to operate and improve the implemented systems in a post-Go-Live environment. Delivery Model rounds out the top six, and addresses the nature of how the integrator will deliver on the project.

Notice how the longer-term elements slip to the back burner once the focus is on delivery. Things like adherence to vision, planning for the post-Go-Live environment, and measurement all take a back seat to getting it done. Later in this book, Michael Doane presents the SAP wedding and SAP marriage mentality. The fact that clients leave longer-term elements on the back burner is evidence that they are focused on the wedding.

Let's go back to measurement for minute. How do organizations quantify the benefits they're deriving from their SAP implementation? They measure it. Note where measurement falls on the list once the project begins. Keep looking, it is way down there near the bottom. Forget measurement, just get it done.

This is mentioned a bit tongue in cheek, as clearly you want the delivery team to be focused on delivering. But it is interesting to see how priorities change once the delivery process starts.

Following these numbers shows that buying teams should continue to place a strong emphasis on understanding the methodology and tools that a systems integrator will follow during the implementation process, as it will be critical to a project's success. Assessing talent can be difficult and the players can change over a long engagement. What remains is the process – make sure you understand it and that it is a good one.

Also, measurement does not just happen. It is part of nearly every step your organization takes throughout the delivery process. Don't be tempted to skip important steps to keep on schedule. It is as important to measure before the project starts as it is to measure after the implementation. Imagine sitting around the conference table with the Chairman of the Board, who is thanking you for all the metrics you just presented, with just one more question: "We just spent $50 million. How much did we improve?" If you skipped the initial measurement to keep on schedule your answer might be, "I don't know." Probably not what the CEO was expecting $50 million later.

## Common Pitfalls of SAP Projects

Implementing SAP is much like a baseball game. The game keeps you on the edge of your seat, the situation can change in a heartbeat, and sometimes it appears there is no end in sight.

If the world were perfect, it wouldn't be.
Yogi Berra

To further the analogy, the project manager can represent the catcher, who must always know the situation, what pitches are working and which ones aren't, and the strengths of the opposing batters (consider these the obstacles faced during an implementation).

Sometimes even when the catcher calls the right pitch and the pitcher throws it perfectly, the batter can drive the ball to the gap. In other words, problems happen.

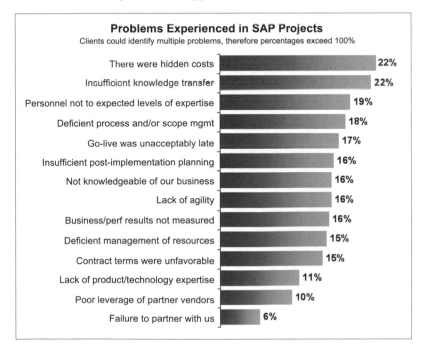

**Problems Experienced in SAP Projects**
Clients could identify multiple problems, therefore percentages exceed 100%

| Problem | Percentage |
|---|---|
| There were hidden costs | 22% |
| Insufficient knowledge transfer | 22% |
| Personnel not to expected levels of expertise | 19% |
| Deficient process and/or scope mgmt | 18% |
| Go-live was unacceptably late | 17% |
| Insufficient post-implementation planning | 16% |
| Not knowledgeable of our business | 16% |
| Lack of agility | 16% |
| Business/perf results not measured | 16% |
| Deficient management of resources | 15% |
| Contract terms were unfavorable | 15% |
| Lack of product/technology expertise | 11% |
| Poor leverage of partner vendors | 10% |
| Failure to partner with us | 6% |

Even with a strong focus on the financial aspects of the SAP project, the number one problem faced when implementing SAP is hidden costs. Work items that weren't originally included in the project plan are typical hidden costs that were mentioned. These include custom modifications, applying more resources to areas of the implementation that were outside the project plan, and travel expenses.

The good news is that most systems integrators will work with customers to address this type of issue. They may not drop all of these costs, but most are willing to come to terms with their clients.

A word of caution regarding fees: when project scope expands, clients are rightfully on the hook for additional fees. Thus, mastery of the engagement's scope at the outset of a project is extremely important, and clients should not presume that unspecified scope will be covered by the systems integrator.

Two other problems found at the top of the standings are insufficient knowledge transfer to end users/team and insufficient post-implementation planning.

Organizations undertake SAP projects because they have specific goals in mind, such as cost reductions, process improvements, or updating legacy systems. Attaining these goals goes beyond the installation of new systems. Organizations need people that can effectively utilize the systems to see demonstrable gains. Oftentimes organizations are so focused on timeframes and budgets that they neglect to properly train their employees. Some clients said things like "after the software was installed we turned around to talk about training our users and nobody was there." When it comes to training your employees, plan ahead.

As mentioned earlier, organizations place a strong emphasis on choosing their provider based on the differentiated strength of the provider's delivery team. Still, one in five didn't get what they thought they paid for. Make sure you meet the project manager – ideally the project manager would be an active participant in the provider's final presentation. Ask the proposed project manager about their specific experience working on project's similar to yours. Use technical jargon typical of your industry and see what type of response you get. If you are comfortable with a particular project manager, build that person's name into the contract so you don't get fooled with a bait-and-switch.

## Goals and the Problems that Hinder Them

In an ideal world your organization wouldn't make any mistakes along its SAP journey, but that is not likely. Two-thirds of organizations report they experienced some type of problem along the way.

> We made too many wrong mistakes.
> Yogi Berra

Not every problem, however, has the same consequences. SAP is about delivering value to the organization – attaining the goals set forth by the steering committee. Our research measures how well clients met their goals (or not).

To answer the question, "which mistakes do we know we don't want to make?" We compare two groups of study participants – those that experienced each problem and those that did not. Because goal attainment is studied as well, goal attainment levels are compared between each of these two groups.

The chart on the following page shows the increase in overall goal attainment when a problem is avoided. As you can see, you don't want to make the "wrong mistakes."

The top three problems with the greatest impact on goal attainment relate directly to the skill set of the integrators people – lack of product / technology expertise, personnel not to expected levels of expertise, and provider not knowledgeable of our business.

Clients had it right when they placed a strong focus on methodologies and tools (most frequently cited differentiator) and the consultancy's technical capabilities (4th highest differentiator) as problems in these areas are the top goal killer of SAP projects.

Where clients mis-directed their attention in the buying process was focusing on reputation and past experiences. Stronger focus on an integrator's consulting skills (rated 8th among differentiators) and related industry experience (rated 10th) play a critical role in attaining goals.

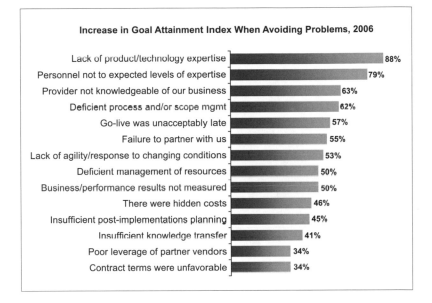

**Increase in Goal Attainment Index When Avoiding Problems, 2006**

| Problem | % |
|---|---|
| Lack of product/technology expertise | 88% |
| Personnel not to expected levels of expertise | 79% |
| Provider not knowledgeable of our business | 63% |
| Deficient process and/or scope mgmt | 62% |
| Go-live was unacceptably late | 57% |
| Failure to partner with us | 55% |
| Lack of agility/response to changing conditions | 53% |
| Deficient management of resources | 50% |
| Business/performance results not measured | 50% |
| There were hidden costs | 46% |
| Insufficient post-implementations planning | 45% |
| Insufficient knowledge transfer | 41% |
| Poor leverage of partner vendors | 34% |
| Contract terms were unfavorable | 34% |

Gaining access to the project team can be difficult during the buying process – more than likely a provider's A-team will be delivering on another client's projects. Just the same, clients should use the leverage they have in the selection phase to require a face-to-face with the key members of the team. Have your best technical people vet their qualifications. Demand that you get reference clients with similar project requirements and ask the difficult questions.

The numbers tell us that no SAP project goes 100% smoothly and that no amount of preparation will ever be enough. The best you can do is your best (that didn't come from Yogi!) – but listen to the voice of 301 customers that have walked this path.

Focus on a provider's methodologies and tools. Meet the project team and grill them about their related experiences. Make sure to properly train your employees. Don't skip important steps to save time in the short term. The extra innings are the ones that matter most.

## Small and Mid-Market SAP Considerations

Of the 301 SAP projects, 92 were completed by small market companies – those with less than $1 billion in annual revenue. Thirty-four of those were among companies with between $300M and $500M in revenue.

As most enterprise application experts will tell you, the small market has slightly different needs than larger companies. Therefore, their perspectives are different from the larger organizations when approaching their SAP project.

Smaller companies evaluate systems integrators slightly differently than larger organizations. Thirty percent of companies with revenue in the $300M - $500M range selected their consultancy based on reputation. This is approximately 50% higher than the overall average. Twenty-five percent of all companies used a consultancy's methodologies as a differentiating factor in their selection decision. Only 17% of clients in this same revenue band indicate methodology was key decision factor in their selection decision.

The good news in their evaluation of providers by these small companies is that they focus on a provider's vertical industry expertise and performance measurement capabilities at approximately double the rate of the industry average.

As the mindset changes to delivery, smaller companies place a stronger emphasis on their partner's consulting skills. This emphasis yields results, as small companies are less likely to be surprised by quality of personnel that their consultancy assigns to their project.

Small companies seem to place themselves a bit at risk by over-emphasizing reputation and de-emphasizing a consultancy's methodologies and tools. Placing a similar focus on a provider's methods that is applied to vertical industry experience and performance measurement is suggested.

# CHAPTER 4

# Are You Ready for SAP?

❑ Red Light, Green Light

❑ Assessing Your SAP Readiness

# Are You Ready for SAP?

## Red Light, Green Light

Over the past ten years, I have provided assessments of firms' readiness to launch an SAP implementation. The firms that have opted for such an assessment are few and far between as the tendency is to presume that with a little bit of reading and lots of dialogue with a systems integrator, all is well.

What I tend to find in the firms that do undertake an assessment:

1. Senior managers presume that company vision and strategy relative to SAP is understood by all business entities.

2. Business staff assigned to SAP implementations, usually for the business process design (blueprint) phase, presume that their role in the project ends at the point of Go Live, if not before.

3. All groups presume that after Go Live the SAP installation will be maintained by the IT organization.

4. IT managers presume that organizational change management applies only to the business units and not to their organization as well.

5. Business staff that is not involved in the implementation project presumes that only end users will be affected once Go Live occurs.

The consequences of poor readiness coupled with these erroneous presumptions are borne out in consequent implementation projects.

Not every firm is capable of successfully carrying out an SAP endeavor. Indeed, many firms have a structure, a culture, or a management style that will sabotage any such undertaking.

Between the poles of "red light" and "green light" are several shaded hues and hard questions need to be honestly answered.

**Company Strategy:** Do you have one? Is it really a strategy, or is it just a list of resolutions and good intentions?

**Your Current Applications:** Are you in a disaster mode or are your current applications simply insufficient? (Note: it is easier to digest an SAP project if your current systems are awful. There's a lot less moaning amongst the ranks about losing the 'good old' systems.)

**Company Structure:** Is your company coherently structured with clear reporting lines and authorities? A test: how long does it take you to explain your company structure to someone from the outside? If more than ten minutes, you may have a problem (and it may be a problem that such a project will help unravel).

**Employee Readiness:** How eager will the employee populace be if you announce that you are going to re-engineer your business processes and implement SAP to support a new organization?

By the same token, do you have sufficient employee expertise for such an evolutionary step?

**Company Attitude re Systems:** Are there any Smith Corona typewriters in your office? How about a Rolodex? Adding machines, punch cards, carbon paper? Do vast numbers of your employees think a CD tray is a cup holder? If you are moving from largely manual and batch systems to SAP, a serious education bridge will have to be crossed.

**Management Style:** How wide is the gulf between senior management and the basic employee populace? Ivory towers are brought low by an SAP project. How cohesive are your management groups? Lack of consensus (and/or discipline) will turn an ASAP project into Project Infinity. (Psst...blame the consultants.)

**Financial Posture:** Cutting corners on an SAP project is ill-advised.

**Recent Company History:** If your company has successfully completed other major projects in the past three or four years, you may be in a strong position to undertake this one. If your company is incessantly launching and dropping initiatives, think again. (As mentioned earlier, the classic cost driver for SAP projects is the start-stop-restart cycle of companies that do not know beforehand what they are getting into.)

Some firms, finding themselves unprepared for an SAP project, take four to six months or longer to attack their weaknesses and then begin. Such preparation, usually education-based, is time well spent and the investment pays off in spades once the project has begun in vigor.

## Very Green Light

Global firms that have struggled with knotty problems like multi-level accounting, language, consolidation nightmares, currency differences, and the like tend to leap to SAP because it addresses those problems head on.

Firms that are facing extinction can succeed because the sense of urgency lends impetus to decision-making, compromise, and the radical change that SAP can foster. Dithering, tinkering, dabbling, and putzing around are not options for firms on the brink of failure.

New firms (i.e. less than ten years old) tend to have flexible employees and fewer stultifying traditions to hold them back.

Firms with unified management whose members share a profit motive (e.g. partnerships) tend to understand the benefits of workflow and react favorably to launching a project that will enable it.

Firms with managers who are unanimously fed up with a long cycle of failed IT projects (perceived or real) tend to look favorably on SAP as an alternative to 'all that.' This type of firm slips back toward yellow light status if these managers lose patience too quickly.

Firms that have enthusiastically undertaken other major projects and succeeded at the majority of them are deep green when it comes to SAP. Even those firms that have tended to leap into trendy new business initiatives of dubious value (Total Quality Management comes to mind) will at least have a culture of experimentation and innovation; more so than timorous, conservative firms.

## Assessing Your SAP Readiness

Each firm will necessarily end up with a combination of red and green lights, the mixture of which, on a color-wheel, results in blue.

In order to move into full green, organizations need to first assess their state of readiness in four key areas across five levels.

### Level 1: Strategy

The firm must have an established business strategy and all stakeholders must understand how SAP is going to support that strategy. By the same token, senior management must assign ownership of results and provide the project team a sufficient level of outside consulting assistance. Lack of strategic readiness will lead to a) under-funding of the effort, b) a failure to gain intended benefits and c) a lack of urgency and priority needed to make the implementation succeed.

## Level 2: Organization

Organizational change management is the key activity during an SAP implementation effort. Senior management and project management must be able to communication both horizontally (to assure that new business processes are rational and agreed) and vertically (to assure that all employee levels are informed). An empowered steering committee should be prepared to assure that the firm will adhere to a policy of change as a continuous process.

Firms that are unprepared to accept and manage necessary organizational change tend to a) over-customize the software in order to perpetuate existing business processes, b) overspend during design and configuration phases as a result of communication/agreement breakdowns, and c) view the effort as linear and limited rather than as the first step toward continuous business improvement.

## Level 3: Goals and Measurements

In a 2003 META Group study, we found that the single greatest implementation mistake cited by 266 firms with installed ERP is: "There was no quantifiable measurement of business benefits."

Measurable business benefits should have a higher priority than simple adherence to time & cost and these measurements must be far more explicit than simple bullet-point goals. Key performance indicators (KPIs) are the recommended measurement level and firms should a) measure current performance in regard to major KPIs, b) establish a mechanism for ongoing targeting and measuring of results, and c) communicate the goals to all stakeholders.

Many clients believe that measuring their current performance is either too difficult or unnecessary. These are the kinds of comments I have heard over the past twelve years:

Measurement is too hard
We already have too many KPIs and no one agrees
upon them.
We know things will be better with SAP, so why don't
we just get on with it?
My favorite: Mr. Doane, I don't think we really want to
know.

A failure to establish and maintain rigorous business performance measurement at the outset of an SAP implementation project strips project teams of clear direction and later leaves a firm in the dark as to what returns have been yielded by the investment.

Michael Connor's chapter on "Seizing Business Benefit with SAP" provides considerable detail in regard to what measurement will yield...business benefit.

### Level 4: Consulting & Education

In the course of the implementation project, knowledge transfer from outside consultants to project team members is a major component of longer-term SAP success. Firms that leave key implementation tasks such as business process design and software configuration to outside consultants fail to gain the knowledge transfer needed to maintain the SAP plant after implementation.

In parallel, the roles of end users will be vastly changed as a result of SAP adoption and the organization should have a written plan in place to support employees whose job responsibilities will change significantly with implementation of SAP. The readiness level of end users should also be taken into consideration prior to end user training. Is a firm's end user base already IT savvy and motivated to take advantage of SAP or will the change and technology leap be a dramatic one?

### Level 5: Awareness & Commitment

Though these two elements may seem "soft," any significant lack in their regard will undermine the success of an SAP implementation.

From senior management to project team members to business managers and end users, there must be a full awareness of how SAP will change roles and responsibilities and a common commitment to the endeavor. At the same time, project planning must reflect that commitment in terms of deadlines, budget, and resource.

Commitment must also be reflected by the preparedness of senior executives to approve major process changes, many of which will result in unwelcome role changes for managers.

In addition, firms must assess the quality of the staff being assigned to the SAP implementation project. Committed firms assign top performers (rather than simply 'available' staff) on a full-time basis.

I once asked a CEO how committed he was to his firm's SAP endeavor. His aggressive reply was "I'm twenty million dollars committed."

I somehow doubt that his project was wildly successful.

To understand how "un-ready" another organization was, consider these elements of organizational readiness where the organization did not even score itself as high as 7.5 of a scale of 1 (low) to 10 (high):

- Our SAP team understands the strategy

- We have an SAP strategy linked to our organizational strategy

- The strategy has been communicated across the project organization and stakeholders

- This organization has completed major technology initiatives in recent years

- We are realistic about what it will take to succeed in this endeavor

- Project staff and stakeholders understand how the SAP effort will address the strategy

- Senior stakeholders have assigned ownership of results

The key to this kind of assessment is that when each individual weighs in you can identify disparities of response that may not be recognized in the course of day-to-day preparation. These disparities will definitely exist between individuals and, more importantly, across defined groups (business management, IT, project team). For example, we are no longer surprised to find that a firm claiming readiness will later reveal that when it comes to strategy, the C-level types give high scores and the project team offers low scores.

The result of your readiness assessment should be an accurate diagnostic of what needs to occur to reach a ready state.

The diagnostic will most probably point to a combination of greater senior management awareness and alignment, more SAP education, and (here's the hard part) organizational changes. Later in the book, we will cover organizational change management, at the heart of which is scaling the power curve that kicks in during any SAP implementation.

# CHAPTER 5

# SAP in a Microwave

❏ A New System Life Cycle

❏ SAP in a Microwave

❏ Post Implementation: The Windfall

❏ Accelerated SAP Implementations

# SAP in a Microwave

## A New System Life Cycle

One of the pre-eminent challenges for information systems people has traditionally been the prolongation of the useful life of an implemented system. "Useful life" may have a malleable definition, but should generally be viewed as "serving the base requirements of the company" (minimum) to "providing business impetus, direction, and economy" (paradigm).

Major IT investments are often followed by major upheavals in a business climate and systems have seldom been updated or enhanced to reflect those upheavals. Thus, the speed of degradation of performance has increased as business complexity has increased.

The life cycle of an information system has traditionally been viewed as circular, as illustrated in the upcoming chart.

In most projects, the degradation of usefulness begins during the acquisition/development stage. The lag time between project planning (when goals and objectives are finalized and hopefully quantified) and implementation can be anywhere from three to twelve months, during which time the business environment will have changed, sometimes radically. Project scope is seldom updated to address those changes and the implemented systems tend to be a source of disappointment.

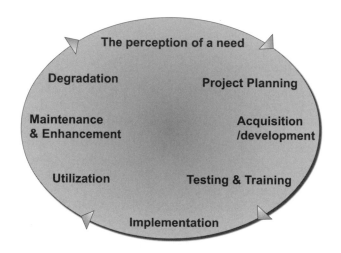

A second, continual phase of degradation begins once the implementation is completed and the system is moved into maintenance mode. Programming alone cannot keep pace with business changes (and consequent changes in needs), most especially because the business changes in question will have an impact on system architecture and interfacing. The IT burden is therefore complicated by functional requirements, integration requirements, and information requirements. It is not surprising that traditional IT cannot meet these expectations.

Degradation occurs when information systems no longer match company needs. Needs change as business changes. These needs can scarcely be met with traditional IT methods.

With SAP, however, this lifecycle does not have to be followed. Instead, a cycle of continuous business improvement can be envisioned. The SAP infrastructure can be modified by business people according to business changes *as they occur* with considerably less delay and disappointment.

Once SAP is implemented, the system should no longer follow this pattern.. Add-on modules and upgrades will always be needed, just as there will also be a "wish list" of functionality that could not be implemented in the core project.

For the core of your business (and a large core at that) you should not find it necessary to redesign or replace software. As needs arise and the performance of the system is found wanting, your company may find it advantageous to re-engineer the business processes that were the model of the initial implementation and reflect changes in the SAP configuration.

## Continuous Business Improvement Cycle

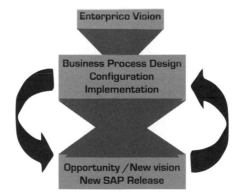

Enterprise Vision

Business Process Design
Configuration
Implementation

Opportunity / New vision
New SAP Release

This should best be a continuous process just as business is a continuous process. Many firms make the mistake of implementing SAP, throwing a Friday night party, (oh those wild SAP parties!) and then stopping on Monday, on the faulty assumption that they now have all they need in the world of information systems. Once implementation is complete, teams are disbanded and SAP efforts are converted into maintenance. This maintenance mentality should be avoided at all costs. SAP should not be maintained like some Cobol-based information system. It should continue to evolve *just as your business evolves*, in the same fashion, at the same pace. Company reorganizations, the incorporation of new distribution methods, emerging markets, acquisitions and mergers, all have an effect on the information system. As configurable software, SAP allows for a rapid response to changes in business climate and degradation of information services should not occur.

The term "implementation" can be misleading. In traditional systems projects, the implementation was the end point in which the new system began to function in place of the old and thereafter only maintenance and enhancements were required. However, an SAP endeavor, embracing business process re-engineering and the installation of integrated enterprise-wide software should necessarily lead to a new life cycle in which continuous re-engineering takes place.

In this chapter, we are addressing what should be referred to as "core implementation"; that is, the first implementation of base modules required supporting your business. Whether this is a phased (or rollout) implementation, in which modules or business sectors are put in play sequentially or a big bang (all modules at the same time) is of no import. The point that must be made is that true implementation is no longer finite but core implementation is.

## SAP in a Microwave

The following is not a complete guide for implementation, merely a rapid tour of how a successful implementation will proceed. For the purposes of this exercise, we will stick primarily to the critical path of an SAP implementation project. The education and change management tracks are detailed elsewhere in this book and the technical track is not what this book is about.

As we have pointed out numerous times, SAP ventures do not always follow traditional paths. However, in terms of a core implementation, the traditional Planning, Development, and Conversion stages that existed pre-SAP still apply.

Since the implementation methodologies of nearly all SAP systems integrators generally adhere to SAP's Accelerated SAP (ASAP) methodology, clients will quickly become familiar with the standard road map.

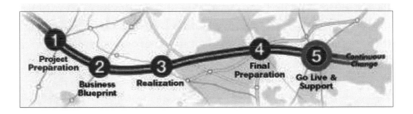

There is one major element missing from this road map: justification. Think of it as phase zero on their road map and phase one on our road map.

### The Planning Stage

The planning stage can be subdivided into these phases:

1. Envision the Future

2. Plan the Venture

3. Gather the Elements

The final two of these coincide with SAP's Project Preparation.

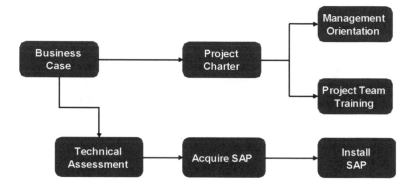

**Phase 1:** *Envision the Future*

At the onset of your endeavor, you should envision the future, justify the means to that future with a business case, and express the vision and the means to project members and employees with a project charter.

We will assume that you have sufficient strategic forces at your disposal to adequately fulfill this task and our purpose here is not to provide guidance for strategic planning. However, one caution begs inclusion: do not let your vision become polluted with mission statements or simple slogans. If you are seeking to trim costs (and head count) while vastly improving your production and positioning yourselves to take advantage of emerging markets, say so. Use tangible terms, not jingoism, or your employee body will doubt the purpose behind the endeavor and your resistance level will be dangerously high.

*Business Case*

Justifying the cost of business systems projects is usually a discomfiting, paper-driven affair in which various individuals are asked to list intended benefits and a clever soul from accounting will gather it all together and pin dollar figures to each of them.

The task here is a cost-benefit analysis and once you have estimated the costs of the project, you should be able to compare them to tangible, measurable benefits as well as those hard-to-define gains, like "improved communications." The business case is a dollars exercise and should provide the financial measuring stick for success or failure.

A later chapter "Seizing Benefits with SAP" provides detail in regard to building a business case. All the same, we will make the point here that far too many SAP investments are made on very shaky business cases. If you are a CIO or project manager, one fast way to get nailed to the wall is to presume that success will be derived simply from bringing your project in on time and on budget.

An acquisition and implementation business case should address:

1. description of the mission (why it is being undertaken and what is the intended result)

2. project priority within the enterprise

3. an assessment of the potential impact on current business for the duration of the project

4. critical success factors

5. anticipated economic benefits and rate of return

6. anticipated strategic benefits and business impact

While most firms adequately develop the first four elements of a business case, the latter two are seldom properly addressed. SAP now offers Value Engineering, which helps clients identify a probable and measurable business benefit and the output of this engineering should be the gravity and direction of your overall business case. The intended amount of your financial return and the timeframe in which it will be realized should be decision drivers during your SAP project planning. Thus you will be able to *plan to benefit* rather than tailoring your plan to time and cost alone.

Note that the business case outlined above is valid not only for firms contemplating an SAP implementation, but also for those that have completed initial implementations and are seeking greater business benefit through time. While we strongly advise any implementing firm to plan to benefit (and not just TCO), we even more strongly advise firms to establish a cycle of continuous business benefit.

## Project Charter

One of the greatest impediments to success in implementing SAP software is the rumor mill. Employees catch wind that an implementation is imminent and a man says he hears it includes "some serious re-structuring" and one woman remembers reading about how SAP is a corporate downsizing tool, and another was once in a company that implemented SAP software and oh, boy there were wall-to-wall consultants.

You get the idea.

You can move ahead of the rumor mill and stay comfortably ahead of it by developing a Project Charter (based upon the

Vision and the Business Case) that will serve as the enterprise definition of the project, stating its aims in an unambiguous and, yes, inspirational manner.

This charter should be signed by the CEO and any members of senior management who are fulfilling the role of project sponsor. It should then be distributed to all employees at the onset of the project. In succeeding months, news of the project (in newsletters, town hall meetings, etc.) should refer to this document and the vision therein to allow for a clear communication of project progress.

Points to be addressed in a Project Charter:

- the name of the project (slogan optional)

- the general aims of the project

- what business entities are involved

- (optional) a master chart illustrating the new enterprise

- the timeframe of the project

- who will be involved - team chart

- why SAP was chosen

- how this will affect the employee populace

- a reminder of past successes.

More and more, consulting firms are providing business case/ project charter services at vastly reduced rates as part of a risk sharing exercise. They do so because a) full project scope is very difficult to identify and freeze prior to completion of this activity, intended business benefits can be properly established, thus facilitating project acceptance by client board of directors, and b) it provides them full opportunity to demonstrate their value at close to cost. This evolution of consulting method is the single most welcome change in recent years and has already contributed to improved success in SAP endeavors.

**Phase 2:** *Plan the Venture*

Because of the new system lifecycle, the planning of an SAP implementation should extend beyond the Day One of system use and should allow for the creation of an organization that will support the new infrastructure and take advantage of the considerable benefits it will afford.

If you are using the ASAP Focus method, a template master plan is already at your disposal. Most systems integrators that do not use at least a variant of Accelerated SAP will have their own template master. Beyond Accelerated SAP, most groups apply the SAP® Solution Manager. Here is how they describe it:

> SAP® Solution Manager is a centralized solution management platform that provides the tools, the integrated content, and the gateway to SAP that you need to implement, support, operate, and monitor your SAP solutions. It helps to minimize risks and to reduce total cost of ownership (TCO). SAP Solution Manager runs in your solution landscape and facilitates the technical support of your distributed systems.

This is a very valuable toolset that is unique, among software vendors, to SAP. If your systems integrator is not using it, you have very possibly chosen the wrong systems integrator.

At any rate, do not use planning templates for traditional IT implementations. They will only lead you astray.

Refine and revise the plan at various points throughout the project, especially if you are working in a large organization and/

or if the project duration exceeds six months. No matter how efficient the team proves to be, by the third month of any project, circumstances will have changed. Plowing ahead *as planned* is not always wise.

Most important of all, plan with realism in mind. Project plans that are molded more by company attitudes and good intentions result in projects that are 'late' and 'over budget.' Projects planned according to realistic assumptions tend to come in under both time and budgetary wires.

**Phase 3:** *Gather the Elements*

With a Project Charter and a Master Plan in hand, you are now prepared to form your team and acquire and install your software.

*Form Your Team*

The key elements of an engagement are:

- Leadership (engagement sponsor and steering committee)

- Delivery team (project Management, internal consulting, external consulting, technical support.

- Framers (organizational change management, quality assurance, and trainers)

- Stakeholders (business people with a direct stake in the outcome.)

Of these elements, **project management** is the most important because the other elements will reflect the manager's vision and expertise. Your firm should name a project manager who possesses a broad understanding of your business (along the horizontal plane) and support this manager with a steering committee or a sponsor from the ranks of senior management.

When an external consulting group is chosen, there will probably also be a project manager included in the mix. Many companies have been successful pairing an internal project manager with an external project manager, whose role is to guide the project through planning and the bulk of development and then turn over the keys to the client. Even if the external project manager is not assigned full-time, it is wise to have someone that your project manager can rely upon for guidance.

For implementations of a long duration, it is normal for some of the team members to leave before the job is done. It can be disastrous if the project manager is among them, so seek to name someone whose presence can be confirmed.

A team of **internal consultants** should be drawn from your ranks and assigned full-time to the project. In smaller firms, this cannot always be accomplished so the project plan must take part-timers into account.

David Chapman of Lyondell-Citgo stresses that a smaller core team with widespread enterprise participation is better than a large core team and little participation: "It is not just a matter of an implementation team 'doing it' and then letting the others in on it. There is a change in depth and breadth, a change of behavior and a change of roles throughout the enterprise. If you cannot foresee acceptance of this across the company body, you might be better off postponing anything more than incremental steps."

The internal team will be matched with the **external consulting** group for development and implementation of the SAP modules chosen. The ratio of internal to external staff will depend upon the quality of staff you assign internally. If you are just grabbing available bodies, you will need more external consultants. If you assign the best and the brightest, you can lower the external consulting level, and if you also accent the transfer of SAP knowledge, you can reduce the duration of the external consultants' stay.

Jon Reed, a longtime SAP recruiter and now an SAP analyst, has this perspective: "SAP consultants with outstanding communications skills as well as strong technical or functional skills tend to be expensive, but pay for themselves by finding a way to 'duplicate' their talents on the project. So-called 'soft skills' do matter."

The criteria for choosing external consultants will be covered in a later chapter. Your choice of internal consultants will hinge upon your ability to 'sacrifice' good people to the project. This can be painful and will clearly have an impact on current business. Further, when the assignments are made, think of many of them as permanent. You cannot assume that at the conclusion of a core implementation that a) the people assigned will wish to return to their old jobs, b) that their old jobs will still exist, or c) that they will still be in your company.

Your **technical support** staff will be a combination of your existing IT group and some outside help for Basis tuning and administration and, possibly, some ABAP/4 programming. The level of support you require will correlate to the number of legacy systems you feel the urge to retain (i.e. interfacing), how much add-on programming you have put onto the menu, and the number of operational sites you are dealing with. Your IT staff will already be skittish about a conversion to SAP, so this may be a sore point. Either your RPGIII programmers are bailing out or they are asking for ABAP/4 training.

## Accelerate Your Knowledge Transfer

At this point in the endeavor, it is imperative that the internal project team accelerate efforts to learn the necessary skills. It is equally imperative for senior management to gain an understanding of what is about to occur and what behaviors are expected of them if it is going to succeed.

These elements are detailed in the chapter "Learning to Swim in the SAP Sea."

## Acquire and Install SAP Software

In most cases, you will be ordered a version that is "pre-configured" to your industry and your country. What this means, in essence, is that the settings and environment are not totally vanilla. For example, the core currency field for a U.S. firm will be set to USD (U.S. dollars); for a French firm, it will be set to Euros.

It would also be wise to hire a solid middleware consultant to assist you in an assessment of your needs before you start ordering hardware. The platform suppliers will have some Basis background, but you would do better to have a third party advising you.

Do not delay for too long your acquisition and installation. While this occurs, your project team should be off educating themselves in regard to software configuration.

At the conclusion of this stage, your staff will have acquired considerable SAP knowledge and you will notice that the software will not perform every business function that you require. Consider the shortfall to be a 'Preliminary Gap Analysis,' but do not leap to fill those gaps with either additional software acquisition or plans for ABAP/4 add-on programming. Many of these perceived gaps will prove to be illusory as the project progresses and your knowledge of the software deepens.

## The Development Stage

The development stage can be subdivided into three phases:

1. Refining the Vision

2. Configuring to Prototype

3. Technical Development

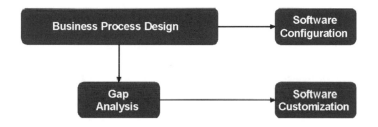

**Phase 1:** *Refining the Vision Through Business Process Design*

The project charter offers headlines, but you will need more details before pouring your efforts into configuring software to "meet the vision."

Refining the vision is a major step in business processing re-engineering. The degree to which you wish to re-engineer your enterprise will determine the complexity and duration of this phase. Will you radically change your ways or will change be more gradual?

Years ago, Calvin Griffith, at the time the owner of the Minnesota Twins, opposed the dramatic rise in baseball salaries by shuffling established stars off to other teams and bringing up newer, rawer, cheaper talent from the minor leagues. His method of tinkering annually left the Twins with the lowest salary level in baseball, but the Twins were often in the middle of the league standings at season's end. Two points of view emerged amongst baseball watchers:

**The Calvin Griffith Upside View:** He had the best return on investment (wins per dollar) of any owner in baseball.

**The Calvin Griffith Downside View:** While other owners were playing to win baseball championships, Calvin Griffith was engaged in a game of pitching pennies and was pleased to go home with a losing record and a five buck profit. (This was, of course, the view of Twins fans).

When it comes to re-engineering your business processes, you will have to make a decision that hinges on just this point: Are you looking for incremental improvements that will strengthen your existing processes or will you seek something more radical by looking at your business with new eyes?

In order to refine the vision, you should consider the major business processes of your firm and imagine how they might be radically improved. An example of a major process is order fulfillment. Order entry, as a subset of order fulfillment, is usually a minor process. Most firms can break down the spectrum of their activity into less than a dozen major processes and these can be analyzed both separately and collectively. In some cases, one new process may replace multiple existing processes.

Remember that your destination is workflow. If you need refreshing on this, return to the latter pages of the chapter "What Is SAP?" The greatest enemy of workflow is the attitude of "this is how we do it here." If how you do it there is so hot and your futures are all assured, you do not need SAP, but you might need a reality check.

One phase that you should spend little time worrying about is the classic AS-IS (aka How We Work Today). There are implementation methods that stress lengthy AS-IS phases, during which your current processes are charted and scripted to infinite detail. The point is that once you have a complete inventory of all you are, you will see clearly what has to be improved. This is bullroar, and costly bullroar if you assign a full-blown AS-IS to a consulting firm. (We think of a full-blown AS-IS phase as "The Consulting Partner's Retirement Fund Phase.") All you truly need is some charting and scripting of current major processes and maybe some of the more complex sub-processes. This exercise will help the external consultants understand your business and the internal consultants learn charting and scripting. Then you can all wash your hands of the chore and get on with the refining of the vision.

A client once ranted that he did not believe at all in "best practices." He asked me whether there was some committee in Germany where various processes were scored by experts and if so, who were these people?

My reply: Bear in mind that you should not be white-boarding as you go through the blueprint phase. All of the leading SAP systems integrators as well as SAP itself have a treasure trove of business processes in their various repositories. We recommend that you take advantage as much as possible of these repositories wherein the "best" practice will be the one that drives the most value for your organization.

## Phase 2: *Configuring to Prototype*

This is where your BPR rubber hits the SAP road, as your team seeks to configure the software to meet the new business process designs. There are hundreds and hundreds of potential tables to be set and their interaction is not negligible, so it is very much a Rubik's cube. You do not want your team engaged in an iterative trial and error process in which you find yourselves moving between design and configuration across all modules until you are satisfied. Such a process will drain your budget and strain your nervous system. You should seek, where possible, to adopt best practices, especially those that are pre-configured.

What this means is that your organization will change to fit the system. This is, of course, not intuitive. Most firms believe that the software should be bent to fit their chosen processes. In some cases, this is a necessity but in many other cases it is simply organizational vanity.

In this light, it must be noted that this is not an either/or situation. Smart SAP clients will adopt an existing (and pre-configured) best practice and simply tweak it where customization is a real requirement.

The re-engineering-configuration loop is the point at which many implementations have bogged down. As the project team seeks to match the configuration to target business practices, the trial-and-error configuring can go on too long. In addition, team members learn more about the vast possibilities of SAP software and can be tempted to add unplanned functionality. This temptation leads to expansion of scope (nothing as slow as scope creep) that also can bog down your progress.

Here are two very good rules to establish when you hit the configuration phase:

**The 48-Hour Rule:** as your configuration team comes to decision points regarding business processes, they will raise them to the client leadership team (process owners and/or project management). An answer or decision must be forthcoming within that time or the configuration team will make up its own mind about what to do. This rule does more to accelerate projects than any other factor and has been proven through hundreds of projects. Use it.

**The Rule of Three:** if your configuration team tries to configure to a given business process and has run three various iterations without success, you should drop whatever part of the process is blocking you. Give it up and walk away. A noted CIO, Bruce Blitch, refers to this as "listening to the software" and accepting its superior wisdom in regard to business processes.

Both of these rules fly in the face of traditional thinking about software in which business people presume to know just how their business should be run. Well, they do not particularly, and often the core logic behind SAP will reject them. So, yes, we are saying you should change your process to fit the software.

And if you cannot?

It is at this juncture that a viable gap analysis can be accomplished. You will find that despite the vastness of the software, it may not address all of the processes in the way you need it to. For each of the identified gaps, your options are:

| Option | Advantage | Disadvantage |
|---|---|---|
| Acquire additional software | Sounds keen | Interfacing and lack of integration |
| Customize away | You get just what you want | You face support and maintenance problems |
| Accept the gap and adapt your process | Retain integration; no interfacing or maintenance; await functional upgrade | Living with the gap; for how long? Is it really a gap? |

There are difficult decisions to be made and the scope of your project may be altered.

Another school of thought is that this point is too late in the project to complete the gap analysis. From here to the end of the project there may not be enough time to fill the gaps, thus compromising the deadline as well as team harmony. We have no quarrel with this school of thought except that experience has taught us that it is truly during the BPR-configuration exercise that real gaps are identified. Users tend to cling to traditional ways of doing business and will negatively compare the new business processes to their current operations. When a gap analysis takes place prior to prototyping, all kinds of misperceived gaps are identified, and more time and money are wasted than if a firm waits until this point.

A re-engineering-configuring loop. Expansion of scope. A gap analysis. This is where the project manager will make the great difference between failure or success. There are compromises to be made and decisions that will not be universally applauded. Weak management at this point will imperil the overall project. But remember that after core implementation you will still be able to configure and re-configure the software, so those elements that fall by the wayside now may be recovered at a later time.

One last note on the subjects of scope and focus:

Normally, you will want to address project scope that will lead to immediate, dramatic benefits, but with limited resources, you may find yourselves accelerating in areas where project ownership is established while getting blocked in areas where project ownership is fuzzy. Says David Chapman, "It is a fact that some of your project impetus will depend upon who from your organization jumps into the project and who does not."

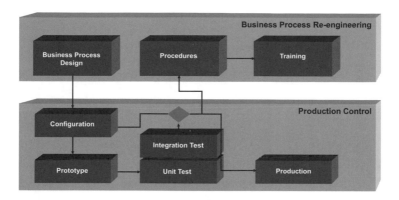

## Plan Your Testing

Nancy Bancroft, author of "Implementing SAP R/3," urges people "to include plans for testing and support systems early in the process. I know we have enough trouble trying to get them to think about training early on, but it is important to plan for testing and support as well. I know of one company that planned a month for testing, but the inevitable happened and they found themselves with only a week before the planned Go-Live for data testing. So they tested for a week and went live with a long list of problems. Of course they immediately started to work on the fixes, but other problems cropped up as the users tried to process their transactions. This company is considering suing their implementation partner."

The company mentioned here is also guilty of planning to deadline rather than planning to completion. The dual point is that a) testing is not a last minute final check; it is a major component of success and b) if the system test fails, you should not Go-Live, no matter what deadline is pinned to the wall.

### Phase 3: *Technical Development*

Areas to be addressed through programming and Basis work include:

- Interfacing

- Migration - Data Conversion

- Operational Environment

- Customizing

- Reporting

If you are retaining certain legacy systems, even for a limited time, you will still need to write **interfaces** between these systems and SAP. Because of the high degree of integration between SAP applications, this interfacing can be complex and costly.

For legacy systems that are being replaced, you will have to prepare programs to **convert necessary data.** This can be nightmarish at the level of the materials management master file, for example, because much of the data you will need to take advantage of SAP software probably do not exist. Completing a data manifest is a time-consuming administrative chore, not a technical task, but it bears mentioning here because the sheer volume of so many materials master files. A typical firm will have between 500 and 15,000 client master records, between 200 and 5,000 supplier master records, anywhere from 50 to 2,000 product records, and anywhere from 1,000 to 1 million material master records.

As configuration is coming to an end, your hardware platform will be prepared and the **operational environment** put into place at the level of Basis. The "tuning" of your installation will continue as modules are ready and system use commences. If you are in a large firm and will have several inter-operational sites, you should note that Basis becomes a major issue as the sites multiply. Balancing and tuning many-site installations will almost certainly require assistance from solid Basis consultants and possibly SAP itself.

Following a gap analysis, you may choose to **customize** with specific programming. Do so with caution. The software includes certain areas known as "user exits," areas that can be customized without endangering your SAP support. Changes to the software outside of these areas may result in your need to perform new maintenance each time you upgrade to a new version of software. User exits are taken into account for upgrades. The other areas are not.

In this regard, over the past twelve years, the rise of global delivery has led to the bulk of RICEF (Reports, Interfaces, Conversions, Enhancements and Forms) being accomplished remotely (in India, predominantly, but also in Eastern Europe, Canada, Russia, China, and the Philippines). The delivery methodologies of most SAP systems integrators cater to global delivery and such services are now quite mature.

Despite the fact that hundreds of standard reports are included in the package (and despite the fact that tools such as Query and SAPScript allow for the easy creation of further reports), most firms feel compelled to undertake a certain amount of ABAP/4 programming to allow for "special customized personalized I-cannot-live-without-this-listing" reports. We are convinced that there is something seriously askew in the world of business when it comes to reports, i.e. formatted information. In a coming chapter, we detail various levels of SAP education for your firm.

### The Conversion Stage

Testing and training are the primary activities of the conversion stage and both of these activities should occur at multiple levels. Timing becomes a major issue for each of these because much of the training depends upon the testing and successful use of the new software, which requires that day one utilization occur shortly after the completion of training.

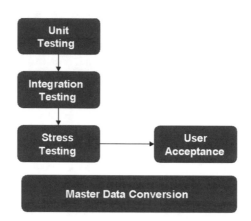

*System Testing*

In simple terms, there are four levels of system testing that must take place.

- Module Testing
- Integration Testing
- Stress Testing
- User Acceptance Testing

**Module testing** actually occurs repeatedly during the configuration process, but a formal and final test of each configured module will still reveal wrinkles that need ironing.

Complete business processes are tested in **integration testing**, which reveals discrepancies between across the ensemble of modules involved in a business process. Similar to the BPR configuring loop, you may find yourselves caught in a testing-reconfiguring loop.

**Stress testing** involves loading the system with more data and more transactions than you will be using. If system performance degrades, Basis help may be required or you may have to tinker with the configuration. Another level of stress testing is to throw wild business scenarios into play (several conflicting sales order modifications, a confusing pattern of delivery requests, etc.) to see whether the system breaks down.

Once the others are satisfied, **user acceptance testing**. To this point, all of the testing will have been done by the system builders, but as users settle themselves into their cockpits and take the system out for a test spin, elements that system builders (who are not users) did not consider will come to light. If super users had little participation in or knowledge of business process design, it may even be wise to run some user acceptance testing prior to the other testing levels.

## Management Preparation

You should envision an effort to prepare management for the imminent conversion to the new system. This does not have to be the object of a formal course or seminar. However, you should communicate how the rhythm of work is about to change and continue to stress the importance of continual business improvement (i.e. that even after day one use of SAP, the evolution will continue and probably accelerate).

## End User Training

How end user training should occur is covered in Chapter 6: "Learning to Swim in the SAP Waters."

The timing of end user training is almost as important as the quality of the training delivered. Wonderfully executed courses will keen the enthusiasm of users, but that enthusiasm will wane and the lessons will be forgotten if there is too lengthy a lull between the training sessions and actual system use.

The finest SAP trainer I know, Patti Walsh, tells people that as far as she is concerned, SAP means Sit and Play. She always makes time to allow her students to "sandbox," which is like test driving a new car. The more time a user can spend playing with the system, the better. Therefore, try to make the system available to end users outside of the training periods in the hope that they will play with it and, in doing so, become more comfortable with navigation and exploitation.

## Data Migration

Once all testing is completed, it is time to finish data migration, with the most important element being master data.

One question that often arises that is almost impossible to answer is: How much historical data (i.e. transaction data) do we need to carry forward?

A second question may help to frame an answer: how much more costly would it be to convert those data to SAP-ready than it would be to create an interface into a legacy database?

## Go-Live

Overly obsessed with the high cost and long duration of enterprise applications implementations, a high percentage of firms shortchange the implementation process and go live prematurely. The short-term effect is usually a loss of intended business benefit but longer-term negative effects of this decision often haunt these firms for years afterward.

In essence, the attitude is "the till is empty, time is up, might as well go live."

While time and cost considerations for SAP implementations are important, the paramount consideration should be long-term SAP agility as evidenced by an ability to gain continuous, measurable business benefit. Mark Dendinger is a Vice President at VSS with more than ten years of experience with SAP clients. His observation is "when clients are too fixated on time and cost, consultants tend to bypass knowledge transfer and there are far more post-implementation costs than would otherwise exist."

Prior to issuing a green light for ERP Go-Live, firms should be assessed in three key areas:

1. **IT & Business Alignment:**

   *Knowledge Transfer/Competency:* IT and Business staff assigned to support & evolution, especially at the business process level, should have received a thorough transfer of knowledge in regard to current business process design, software configuration, customizations, and methods.

   *Continuity:* Most clients erroneously dissolve the core implementation team shortly after Go-Live and revert to a traditional IT maintenance mode that results in an incremental improvement rut. Instead, a mix of business and IT staff should be retained after the project with the express role of assuring continuous business improvement by which business benefits are targeted and measured, preferably at the level of Key Performance Indicators (KPI).

   *Organization:* Ongoing improvements to business processes are led by business staff and supported by IT.

2. **Infrastructure**

   *Knowledge Transfer/Competency:* IT staff should be prepared to support all infrastructure across the entire enterprise applications portfolio. Many firms tend to plan infrastructure changes only for the SAP portion of the portfolio and later run into adaptation difficulties.

*Continuity:* Plans for process changes, upgrades, or other changes to software should be reflected in an adaptive infrastructure plan.

*Organization:* Process owners and configuration staff must have a direct communications channel to IT infrastructure and operations staff in order to avoid disconnects between business blueprints and operational realities.

3. **End Users**

*Knowledge Transfer/Competency:* End users should have received sufficient training to features, functions, and roles within business processes.

*Continuity:* A continuous training program is funded and attrition/change management procedures are in place as well as sufficient help desk resource.

*Organization:* Ownership, authority, and budget for end user training are established within the organization.

IT/Business Alignment and Infrastructure in a post-go live environment are detailed in the chapter "There's No Such Thing as Having SAP."

The failure of most firms to adequately train their end users will be addressed in the chapter "Learning to Swim in the SAP Sea."

## Post-Implementation: the Windfall

It is always a great pleasure to talk to people who have not only succeeded in implementing SAP software but who also continued to help their firms evolve by *using* SAP software. All of these people admit that they expected to set down their implementation tools once the core implementation was finished, and were surprised to find that there is a continued acceleration of business improvement AFTER the core implementation. In all cases, these people express how gratifying it is to continuously implement in the course of daily business.

Once the core implementation is complete, it is as though you have just nudged your canoe onto a far shore and the destination of workflow is at last in sight.

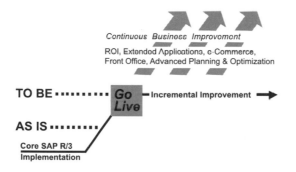

Assuming you have mastered the principle of continuous business improvement, you will find yourselves immersed in ever more beneficial activities. With a working core of SAP software, much of the time pressure should be removed and you will be in a position to go back to gaps that could not be addressed in the first go. Further, through your use of the software, you will identify champions, people who grasp how to take advantage of its features to bring benefit to the firm.

You will also be in a position to consider additional applications that were not included in the core implementation. Applications such as Project System, Quality Maintenance, Plant Maintenance, and Workflow usually fall under this heading.

One post-implementation legacy is the existence of people whose jobs include the management of business processes and the consequent disappearance of "vertical" management (for discrete business units). Process managers, armed with a functioning suite, will continue to tinker with the configuration according to opportunity as well as changing business conditions. If you are in top management, you should not view this re-configuring as a pointless perpetuation of the implementation but see it as the sweetest fruit of the endeavor.

Another post-implementation legacy is that people from heretofore disparate sectors will find themselves working together on a daily basis. Representatives from finance, logistics, production planning, transport, et al, who were thrown together for the implementation, will find that their bond is complete and that ongoing, evolutionary business process re-design and configuration is a part of their new job descriptions.

## Accelerated SAP Implementations

In 1995, the drums of the North American press began to pound out an impatient rhythm: SAP takes an eternity to implement. In 1996, that pounding turned to a steady, *noisy* beat and, in the spring of 1997, SAP America unveiled its new methodology for implementing R/3. It was called Accelerated SAP or ASAP for short. After myriad improvements to this methodology in the intervening ten years, it is now called ASAP Focus.

> I once put instant coffee in a microwave and almost went back in time.
> Steven Wright

ASAP Focus, to its credit, has a rational AS-IS phase and there is a treasure trove of tools that *will* help you to speed up the process, such as a pre-canned project plan, an exhaustive inventory of business processes (related to SAP module chains), and a large number of template forms and procedures. Further, ASAP is built as a Microsoft Office™ kit, including Word documents, Excel spreadsheets, MS Project plans, and PowerPoint slide shows. It is possible to tweak the method by either including other documents or revising those that are offered to suit your needs and context.

Once this methodology was released, consulting firms immediately raced to complete implementations faster and faster and the marketing world was dotted with ads and announcements like "Roadrunner Corporation Completes SAP Implementation During Long Lunch Break!." The five basic steps are:

1. Project Preparation

2. Business Blueprint

3. Realization

4. Final Preparation

5. Go-Live

The chart below provides a thumbnail estimate of the percentage of effort required for each phase.

| Phase | Activity | % of Effort |
|---|---|---|
| Project Preparation | Scoping, staffing, team training, process fit | 10% |
| Blueprinting | Enterprise modeling/business process design | 25% |
| Realization | Configuration & customization/interfacing | 35% |
| Final Preparation | Data migration, end user training | 25% |
| Go Live | Cut-over and support | 5% |
| | | 100% |

Project elements that will accelerate an implementation:

1. Visible, measurable criteria for success

2. Mastery of scope

3. Transfer of SAP knowledge from consultant to client

4. ASAP - for its accelerator tools.

5. Knowledgeable management commitment

Note that 60% of the project is devoted to blueprinting and realization. In the blueprinting phase, a client and systems integrator collaborate to design the over-all enterprise model and then the business processes that will address that model. In the course of this work, there is usually a lot of debate between various client members as to the process design. These debates tend to include arguments such as "that's not how we do it here" answered with "but this is how we should be doing it."

Clients who accept new business processes based on best industry practices can avoid these costly arguments and by consequence vastly reduce blueprinting. When best practices are adopted, configuration is also reduced since the best practice processes are already configured.

Consider the following scenario in which a firm largely adopts best practices but still has some tweaking:

Such adoption is usually far easier for small and medium enterprises and thus fully accelerated implementations occur more often in that arena.

| Phase | Standard Cost | Accelerated Cost | Savings |
|---|---|---|---|
| Project Preparation | $50,000 | $100,000 | - $50,000 |
| Blueprinting | $125,000 | $50,000 | $75,000 |
| Realization | $175,000 | $80,000 | $95,000 |
| Final Preparation | $125,000 | $125,000 | $0 |
| Go Live | $25,000 | $25,000 | $0 |
| | $500,000 | $380,000 | $120,000 |

In such a scenario, project preparation is more costly due to the process validation required to identify which processes can be fully adopted and which will require some process change.

By consequence, blueprinting costs are vastly reduced as are configuration costs since the best practice processes are pre-configured.

The result is a cost savings of 24% with a similar compression in the time to Go-Live.

In essence, the greater the adoption of best practices, the higher the savings. In many, many cases, clients have no blueprinting costs at all.

Says Mark Dendinger of VSS: "The reduction of blueprinting gives impetus to an implementation project. Clients love to see fast results from pre-configured business processes and the acceleration improves team morale."

You may ask, "Where do these best practices come from?" The answer is that they are culled from more than 30,000 clients across seventy industries. In other words, the trailblazing has long since been accomplished, so why would your firm feel the urge to get out machetes to hack new trails?

The bottom line is that adapting to best practices is not a "one size fits all" proposition but a "one way best fits most" proposition.

| Benefit | Enabler |
|---|---|
| Reduced time & cost | Mastery of scope, the deployment of accelerators, and a reduction of business process design |
| Reduced disruption to the client's existing operations | Less client involvement in implementation and shorter duration of disruption |
| Adherence to best practices | More disciplined adoption of best practices with less latitude for business process customization |

SAP provides a frequently-updated chart regarding implementation duration. The most recent chart claims that 61% of all implementations are completed in less than 9 months with the majority of implementations for firms with <$200M in revenues being six months or less.

An SAP solution implemented with the SAP ASAP Focus methodology includes:

❑ A road map defining the shortest route to implementing a pre-defined solution.

❑ Pre-tested processes for specific business activities data conversion tools that allow the project team to validate the solution with your data.

❑ Ready-made documentation covering business processes and configuration. This documentation supports organizational change management efforts.

❑ Predefined reports, print forms, authorization roles, test scenarios, and a variety of templates that all help to accelerate your progress.

It is essential not to lose sight of the fact that the implementation should yield measurable business benefit and readers are strongly advised to precede any such implementation with a Value Engineering exercise that will help to isolate and quantify potential improvements in key performance indicators.

In past years, too many clients opted for accelerated implementations that, quite simply, skipped over organizational change management, foreshortened user training and other knowledge transfer, and raced through data migration with insufficient data cleansing...only to find their time and cost savings eroded by a faulty go-live.

In "SAP by the Numbers," Paul Reynolds presents findings from Performance Monitor's 2007 study of 301 SAP projects which included an inventory of the problems that arose in the course of those projects.

While four of the top six problems relate to the project at hand, the other two "insufficient knowledge transfer' and 'insufficient post-implementation planning,' have long-lasting consequences.

Thus, while this chapter provides an outline as to how an initial implementation will take place, the next chapter provides guidance in regard to what is in store after go-live.

# CHAPTER 6

# There's No Such Thing as Having SAP

❏ The SAP Long Haul

❏ Post-Implementation Excellence

❏ Center of Excellence Maturity

❏ Application Outsourcing

# There's No Such Thing as Having SAP

## The SAP Long Haul

The first version of this book was published in 1998 and the chapter "SAP in a Microwave" was so named because of the contemporary (pre-Y2K) emphasis on speedy implementations. In early 2001, I joined META Group as an industry analyst and one of my first client engagements was with a firm that had implemented SAP three years prior. The client claimed that the implementation had gone fairly well but in the three years since Go-Live they had continually struggled in regard to operations and were unable to get tangible returns from their investment. They said that during the three years it took them to implement SAP that they had spent very little time preparing for post Go-Live and what they asked for was assistance in building an SAP Center of Excellence.

My first reaction was regret in regard to much of my previous advice to clients relative to implementation speed and the fact that this book made scant mention of post-Go-Live planning. My second reaction was to review the methodologies of most of the major SAP systems integration firms: Fast Track™ for Deloitte, Rapid Return on Investment (R²i) for BearingPoint (then KPMG), Accelerated SAP (ASAP) for SAP, and Ascendant for IBM BCS (then PWC Consulting). I found the same paucity of post-implementation planning in all of them. In times since, we have seen considerable improvement in this regard and it is up to clients to understand, and appreciate, and pay for the steps needed to prepare themselves for post Go-Live.

During my four-plus years at META Group, I led a number of studies into the ERP installed base and found that the client in question was not unique as one of the chief regrets of ERP clients was a failure to create a post-implementation organization that could optimize operations and sustain intended benefits.

Not all the blame can be laid at the systems integrator doorstep. Too many clients are overly concerned about the impending cost of an SAP engagement and refuse to add the 3%-5% more in consulting costs that will provide sufficient post-implementation planning. Often, clients are using an antique statistic –Total Cost of Ownership – as the measure of their success.

The life expectancy of an SAP installation is anywhere from twenty to thirty years. If that seems long to you, consider the simple fact that sunk cost alone is a massive impediment to any firm that even considers shifting away from an implemented SAP to something else. Also consider that hundreds of firms have already been running on SAP for twenty-five years.

Given this life expectancy, wise clients will look beyond the implementation costs and provide themselves a proper operating foundation for the long haul.

Here is how most clients plan for SAP costs:

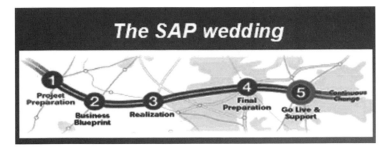

Note that little label on the far right. It is in a smaller font than the labels for the five phases leading up to Go Live. Think of it as the small print in a marital contract, since the cost/duration reality of SAP is more like this.

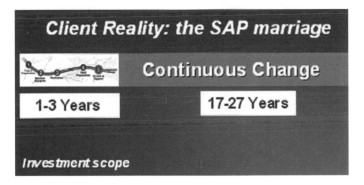

This is why Total Cost of Ownership has lost its utility as a key performance indicator for SAP implementations.

John Leffler, who heads up the global SAP practice for IBM Global Business Services, is one of the leading lights of the SAP universe. When we met in 2001, I asked him how badly market saturation was affecting his business. He smiled and proceeded to list off upgrades, extended applications, optimizations, migrations, global rollouts, and more, and then concluded his response by lifting both arms as if to embrace the world and said, "Michael, there's no such thing as having SAP."

In the intervening years, having seen a number of SAP consulting practices thrive and last year's double-digit growth in SAP software sales, I have used this line, and its depth of meaning, as a touchstone.

## Post-Implementation Excellence

Two key elements have lead directly to SAP disappointment:

1. The "wedding" viewpoint around SAP investments and returns

2. A failure to institute business-based targets and measurements.

Adopting a "wedding" viewpoint leads firms to break up their implementation teams after Go-Live and turn maintenance over to the IT people, as if all that talk about business and IT alignment was meant only for the implementation project.

While a number of key post-implementations properly belong to IT (help desk, technical integration management, database, etc.) business process improvements will not occur on a continual basis if all the business people have gone away.

In order to assure continuous business improvement, readers are advised to create a Center of Excellence at the outset of an initial implementation.

### Create a Center of Excellence

Most clients find that the "To Be" vision developed at the onset of an SAP implementation is not fully realized at the point of Go Live. However, the project is still viewed as "complete" and a major part of the implementation team is disbanded at the same time the systems integrators make their farewells. Such firms quickly find themselves in a rut of incremental improvements and never do attain even the initial "To Be" state.

A Center of Excellence (or competency center) dedicated to continuous business improvement is required. The object of such a center is:

1. An optimization of business processes that drive business benefit

2. An optimization of end user competency and employee fulfillment of business processes

3. Continued coherence and integration of functionality and data through all process chains.

In essence, the "To Be" vision that was created at the outset of an SAP endeavor must be refreshed and pursued on an ongoing basis or the SAP "sunk cost" will remain just that.

The formation of a Center of Excellence can follow a variety of paths, but some absolutes are easily identified and must be inherent: Do not break up the implementation team that was formed during Project Preparation and has gained invaluable experience in business process design, configuration, and enterprise-wide integration skills. Most or all of this team should remain intact for continuous re-design and configuration targeted toward continuing business benefit.

Continuous end user training must be implemented. Degrading user competency is a major cause of lost benefit in the SAP installed base. One round of "end user training" prior to Go-Live will be insufficient within six months.

The Center of Excellence must be "business centric," not IT-centric. In a key white paper written by Thomas H. Davenport, of Accenture's Institute for Strategic Change, an executive from Canada Post is quoted: "We found companies that put Centers of

Excellence in their IT organizations weren't as successful as those who put it in their business-side organizations." ("Enterprise Solutions and Ongoing Business Change," April 20, 2002, Thomas H. Davenport).

The obvious necessity is to drive change through business, not IT. Process owners should be driving continuous improvements and receive strategic marching orders from whoever is monitoring the Key Performance Indicators.

The chart below is but one possible variant for a Center of Excellence.

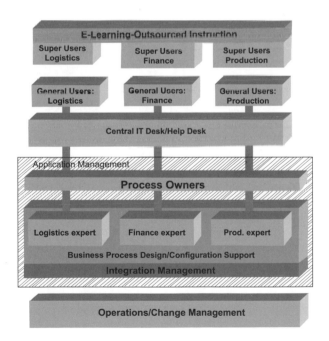

This is a business-centric organization supported by IT.

The bottom line advisory to firms using SAP: You can't have it both ways. If you are not willing to make the organizational and business process changes inherent to an SAP endeavor, you will be forced to customize. If you do not establish measures regarding your business, you will not know whether you are gaining benefit from SAP. If you do not change your business/IT support organization, you will get only incremental and unsatisfactory benefits from your investment.

## Center of Excellence Maturity

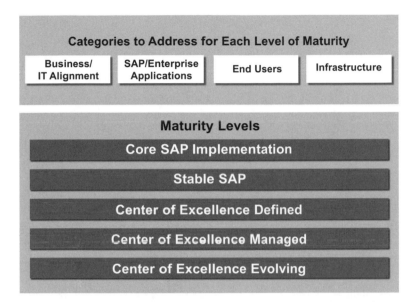

The above table outlines a maturity model for establishing and evolving a Center of Excellence. There are four categories of activity to assess for each maturity level.

The five levels of the model are:

**Level 1: Core SAP implementation:** Clients may attain this level only if the core SAP implementation and at least the majority of corresponding geographic rollouts have been completed, the end users have been satisfactorily trained, and no significant amount of continuing application implementation is occurring. The client has agreed on a combination of processes, lines of business, and geographies to be frozen and hence supported by the CoE. Clients are advised to take a close look at the level of software customization that has been or is still occurring. Customization will negatively impact their ability to move forward, regarding not only the maturity of the enterprise application CoE, but also subsequent upgrades of SAP software or future SAP projects. For the first two maturity levels, SAP is the primary focus since SAP is at the center of the enterprise application portfolio.

**Level 2: Stable SAP:** SAP stability is a combination of end users being functional, infrastructure being adequate, and the interfacing of SAP applications to other related applications generally being in place. An application center of excellence cannot be adequately defined, staffed, and effective if SAP operations remain unstable.

**Level 3: CoE Defined:** This is the "hump" maturity level in which clients must turn the corner from simply operating the installed SAP and move toward an evolutionary state in which the business and the IT group are better aligned. Certainly, the definition of this alignment can happen much earlier, not only at the business process/data management levels, but also at the end-user level. Further, the client must, in this phase, begin to scroll together all enterprise applications, whether vendor-supplied or in-house/legacy. We also recommend that the client engage in an application portfolio rationalization exercise to be sure that after Go-Live the appropriate legacy systems have been retired.

At this stage in the maturity model, a client must have key performance indicators (KPIs) established within systems, including a proper measurement of current actual KPI performance.

**Level 4: CoE Managed:** A managed center of excellence presumes that end users are aware of their role within business processes. It also presumes that business staff members are actively involved in business process analysis and design, have direct roles in enterprise application configuration (where applicable), or have direct authorization over enterprise application software development. At this point in the maturity model, a proper balance will be struck between business-oriented staff and IT staff, in which IT professionals are also highly focused business decision makers centered on business process improvement that will yield measurable business results.

**Level 5: CoE Evolving:** An evolving CoE is immediately responsive to business threats or opportunities, with end users fully participating in business performance across business processes. Business processes are continually improved based on KPIs and enterprise program management strategies. KPIs are benchmarked. The system indicates which transacts impact KPIs. Executive decisions to ameliorate KPIs are tracked in a knowledge management system.

For each of these maturity levels, four areas come into play.

**Business/IT alignment:** A center of excellence is intended to drive business results; therefore, it must also be staffed by business personnel who are supported by the appropriate IT staff. Most firms fail to maintain this alignment due to a reliance on pre-SAP practices in which the IT group alone managed application evolution.

**Enterprise applications:** The state of the applications (software, functionality, reliability, and interoperability) will have an impact on staff members' ability to impact change (business process improvement). Unstable applications, especially those that are highly customized, will consume both IT and business resources with support tasks.

**Infrastructure:** Enterprise applications can be stable only if the hardware/software infrastructural supports are in place. Software infrastructure includes areas like change management and testing (aka "Promote to Production"). An evolving center of excellence will require a state of adaptive infrastructure by which changes to applications are reflected by relevant changes to the infrastructure.

**End users:** These are the people who actually run the business processes delivered by the enterprise applications. Their level of competence, preferably driven by a continuous training program, will have a direct effect on business process performance and a firm's ability to absorb continuous change. Most firms have failed in this regard due to a reliance on SAP end user training practices that ended on the Go-Live date.

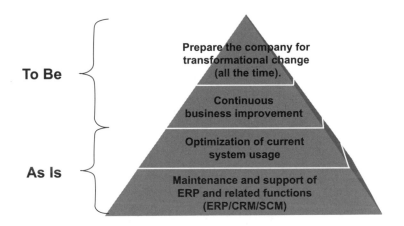

Without a center of excellence, organizations can only address their new As-Is state. With a center of excellence that is business-centric, the future state can be continually addressed.

John Leffler is right; there is no such as having SAP in the sense of "It is ours and it's over."

If this is all too much for your organization, you may be a candidate for application outsourcing.

## Application Outsourcing

A number of firms offer clients the option of outsourcing the management of the applications after Go-Live. This is referred to with varying terms by a number of service providers. Here are our definitions:

**Application Maintenance:** basic applications hosting/operations, break/fix, debug, backup, etc. In short, keeping the SAP lights on.

**Application Management:** maintenance functions (above) plus a level of application improvement, upgrade, and/or business process transformation.

For the latter, there are various levels of management:

- Functional application enhancement as needed to assure basic *continuity*

- Frequent application enhancements to provide some *optimization*

- Defined levels/stages of business process *transformation*

While systems integration is fairly mature for initial implementations, upgrades, geographic rollouts, and optimizations, application outsourcing for SAP is a relatively new and emerging service. While, no reliable statistics are available as to what percentage of the SAP installed base deploys application management, it is presumed that no more than 3% do so, probably less.

One question that has lingered is whether clients can gain value from outsourcing their applications. One obvious lure, dangled by the service providers, is reduced cost of IT but many clients I have spoken with over the past five years tell me that they would accept similar costs if application outsourcing services freed them up to fulfill more strategic tasks. Many more clients claim to be seeking hard-to-find skills or to simply raise the SAP talent level.

In a very recent study based on input of more than 700 clients of eight leading application outsourcing providers, Performance Monitor research includes each client's assessment of their organization's overall goal attainment as well an assessment of eight individual goals. The scale used to evaluate goal attainment is provided below:

❑ Falling Far Short of Expectations (1)

❑ Falling Just Short of Expectations (2)

❑ Meeting Expectations (3)

❑ Slightly Exceeding Expectations (4)

❑ Far Exceeding Expectations (5)

Every client has certain expectations when they make the decision to outsource their applications. While exceeding those expectations is nice, most clients are satisfied so long as their expectations are met. Using the scale above as a guide, a provider will have done their job if the client provides a rating of three or higher. When studying an index across this spectrum, we look for the degree of separation we get from a flat 3.00.

The goal attainment index for more than 700 clients over a four-year period is 3.26. On the next page are the annual results.

## Application Outsourcing Goal Attainment

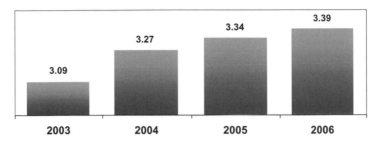

CHAPTER 7

# Seizing Business Benefits with SAP
*by Michael Connor*

❑ At the End of the SAP Rainbow

❑ Show Me the Money!

❑ We Have Met the Enemy and...

❑ It is Getting Better All the Time

❑ And in the End...

# Seizing Business Benefit with SAP

## At the End of the SAP Rainbow

It is undeniable that SAP has delivered billions of dollars of value to its customers. But what do we mean by business benefits? A business benefit results when your operations work measurably better, faster, or cheaper as a direct result of your SAP investment. A specific function, like receiving or accounts payable, may work better; a set of functions might enjoy better integration; it may be as simple as all functions gaining better data with which to work. What matters is you wouldn't enjoy these improvements if you hadn't invested in SAP.

In practice SAP can deliver a range of measurable, hard-dollar benefits and a range of soft, or strategic, benefits. Much of SAP's goodwill today is grounded in its strategic benefits, the feeling SAP customers have that they work better... Our intent is to equip you with the ability to plan, deliver, and measure SAP's hard and soft rewards.

## Show Me The Money!

Let's first discuss SAP's hard-dollar benefits. Hard benefits are highly likely to appear in certain portions of your operations.

❑ In your Finance organization, especially if you use SAP to accelerate your cash cycle (your cash cycle encompasses how cash is tied up in inventory, receivables, and payables).

❑ In your Inventories, including raw materials, work in progress, and finished holdings.

❑ In your Purchasing, especially when you use SAP to increase your buying power.

❑ In your Asset Management, especially if you, like many companies, have lost control over what you own and maintain.

Hard benefits reflect the dollars saved or gained when SAP helps you work more effectively (better), more efficiently (faster), and plain old cheaper. Some examples of the hard benefits organizations have gained from SAP include:

❑ Reduced inventory by 15% compared to last year's inventory levels.

❑ Decreased cycle time by 12% per month.

❑ Cut rework by 100% compared to last month's level of effort.

You can spot hard benefits by the language used to describe them. Hard benefit descriptions always begin with an action verb, have a noun in the middle that can be "dollarized," and end with a data point. Action verbs describing hard benefits include improved, reduced, eliminated, consolidated, streamlined, and avoided.

Items that can be dollarized include cash (of course), inventory, time, and head count.

Consider the following statements:

❏ "Using SAP we reduced our inventory by 15% per annum. It is a hard benefit – you can attach dollars to inventory – and it passes our three-part test: Verb: Reduced. Noun: Inventory. Data Point: 15% per annum.

❏ "Because of SAP we've increased the discounts we take by 25%." It is also a hard benefit – you can attach dollars to discounts gained – and it again passes our three-part test: Verb: Increased. Noun: Discounts. Data Point: 25%.

❏ "With SAP we're twice as efficient as before." Could be a hard benefit, but you need to clarify what "efficient" means – do we do everything at half the time it took before? If yes, what is the value of that time?

❏ "Using SAP we improved operations a lot." Clearly not a hard benefit; what's the dollar value of "a lot"?

Hard benefits are like luck (apologies to Branch Rickey, the baseball executive who broke major league baseball's color barrier by signing Jackie Robinson); they are "the residue of design." You realize hard benefits when you understand what SAP can and cannot deliver. If you tell me you expect to increase gross margins by reducing the materials component of cost of goods sold you are seeking something SAP can deliver. If you say you are going to increase gross margins by increasing prices I'd suggest you have imputed magic powers to SAP that it just doesn't have.

When you are planning the hard benefits you will seek during your SAP implementation, we suggest you brainstorm specific improvements in your business operations and then ask, "Where, when, and how has SAP enabled these improvements?"

Set your standards for a radically different business case, one that identifies operational improvements, quantifies dollars delivered or saved from SAP-driven operational improvements, and specifies the Key Performance Indicators you will use to measure and manage gains. Dollars delivered or saved should come from existing profit-and-loss statements, balance sheets, cash flow statements, and/or operating and capital budgets; otherwise they will not be part of your existing financial reporting framework and will lack credibility and traction. Key Performance Indicators should be designed to credibly and continually prove the hard benefits you are delivering.

Key Performance Indicators, or KPIs, are, well, key simply because it's very difficult to prove you have delivered hard benefits without Key Performance Indicators. We advise you to develop and deploy two types of KPIs during your SAP implementations.

**Business Strategy**
*What are we trying to accomplish?*

**Business Goals**
*What are our supporting short and long-term objectives?*

**Business Drivers**
*What needs to happen to achieve these objectives?*

**Key Performance Indicators**
*What metrics are needed to measure and manage our drivers?*

**Operational KPIs** capture SAP's sustained changes in your business operations that SAP delivers. Annual reduction in order cycle time is an example of an Operational KPI.

The logic behind Operational KPIs is simple. If SAP's functionality allows you to work better, faster, and/or cheaper, you need KPIs to measure the extent to which your business actually operates better, faster, and/or cheaper. Think of KPIs as SAP's proof points—a good thing to have when you are shoveling millions into an SAP platform.

Operational KPIs have long shelf lives. Your implementation of SAP is 25-plus-year commitment. You will use Operational KPIs to both measure benefits and tune your SAP configuration for as long as you run SAP.

Until recent years, too few implementations effectively used Operational KPIs. In our experience most SAP implementations either failed to identify how they expect to change operations, failed to create a baseline measure of business operations, or failed to measure operational improvements once live with SAP. What a waste – CEOs carping about SAP's expense only when someone failed to take the time to adequately develop and deploy Operational KPIs capable of showing SAP's benefits.

SAP drove the subject of IT into the boardroom and happily the clientele have awakened to the need to target and attain measurable business benefit. Toward that end, as mentioned earlier in this book, SAP has for some time been offering Value Engineering by which clients identify and quantify targeted benefits at the KPI level. Once SAP is operational, the movement of those KPIs (e.g. to what point things are or aren't getting better) can be monitored. Ongoing business process changes can now be guided by actual business results.

**Program KPIs** ensure you deliver your SAP implementation on time and on budget and, most important, ensure you deliver the functionality your organization truly needs to work better, faster, and cheaper. Percent of functionality through Level Three testing is an example of a Program KPI.

The logic behind Program KPIs remains simple. You are spending millions (perhaps hundreds of millions) of dollars, dinars, rupees, or pounds on your SAP implementation. Program KPIs let you manage your program's schedule, budget, scope, and manpower prudently and proactively.

SAP programs typically comprise multiple work streams, with each work stream focusing on one or more SAP modules. Program KPIs for an SAP implementation will exist first at the work stream levels and aggregate up to the program level.

Program KPIs typically have a finite shelf life, existing for the duration of the program. This is wrong; the same Program KPIs used during your SAP implementation should, for the most part, be used during your Center of Excellence's ongoing efforts to sustain, upgrade, and extend your SAP platform.

So, we have established that SAP can deliver a range of hard-dollar benefits. We have made especially clear, we hope, that hard benefits result when you smartly plan and deploy your SAP platform.

But we haven't yet addressed the question that nags SAP: Why is there a perception that too many SAP implementations failed to deliver the measurable benefits they hoped to deliver?

## We Have Met The Enemy and...

In truth, the whole area of benefits realized from SAP implementations is a sore subject for many organizations. The vast majority of SAP customers would say they are happy they implemented SAP. But our experience suggests that some cannot point to specific, sustained benefits resulting directly from their SAP efforts.

We observe SAP suffers three problems in the benefits area. None of these problems is intrinsic or special to SAP (or any ERP package, for that matter). Each and every one of these problems is caused by *you.* Let's explore.

SAP's first benefits problem was neatly summarized in earlier editions of this book: "During a lengthy implementation process, the temptation is too often to 'get it over with' and, in such scenarios, benefits go by the wayside." The rush to complete the project, to hit the Go Live date and to run like heck away from your SAP efforts, encourages compromises in the functionality you deliver to end users. Functionality, which represents your company's future ability to do business better/faster/cheaper, is pared from scope faster and faster as hurtle toward your set-in-stone Go Live day. Benefits following Go-Live suffer because, as Gertrude Stein said of her hometown of Oakland, California, "There is no 'there' there"—there is little substantive change in business processes and therefore few ways to do work better/faster/cheaper.

SAP's second benefits problem is what we call "benefits case fiction." A business case is developed with little understanding of what SAP can and cannot deliver. The actual changes realized in the business are the result of on-the-fly configuration decisions – we'll tweak this process, change this decision loop, and batch these data – not strategic decisions about how you want your business to operate. The benefits that result are coincidental to the implementation effort and too often pale in comparison to what they could have been if a true benefits case guided your implementation efforts.

SAP's third benefits problem is what we call "benefits case loathing." Once again a business case is developed, and it might even be solid. But the business side of the organization doesn't understand how SAP will deliver specified benefits, they doubt the credibility of the benefits case, and they consequently refuse to attribute improvements to SAP and, even worse, are loath to reflect SAP's benefits in their capital and operating budgets. Benefits may happen, but they will not be reflected in the documents that matter to the business.

Which leads to an important rule of thumb: if a benefit doesn't show up in your organization's capital or operating budget, it's not a business benefit.

With one BIG exception: a chief benefit derived from implementing SAP is SAP's ability to reduce the complexity of your IT infrastructure and, more important, the complexity of your business processes (if you really have business processes, that is). Most organizations are moving away from total legacy messes when they move onto SAP.

In virtually every implementation we've supported, (and collectively we've supported quite a few), at some early point in our engagement one or more CIO-types will wave their "spaghetti chart" showing their tangled web of legacy systems and exclaim, "We can't support this mess any longer!" The promise of a single, integrated system used by more than 38,000 other organizations worldwide makes it easy for organizations to set foot on the SAP path. And once businesses run on SAP they almost always find they eventually work better.

## It's Getting Better All the Time

We believe organizations should implement SAP; otherwise this would be a darn short book. And we believe your business will run better as a result of running SAP. If you ask SAP to deliver the changes it can deliver, and if you plan your implementation around these proven changes, we have no doubt you will receive hard-dollar benefits from your efforts. We're equally confident you will receive a slew of intangible benefits from your SAP efforts.

"What are these intangible benefits? And why should I care," you might ask.

An SAP AG presentation entitled "ROI Business Case" lists a number of intangible benefits. I've lifted their claims from the presentation (SAP's text is in quotes) and offered our view on promised benefits. SAP's benefits claims are divided into "Slam Dunks" and "Maybes" categories.

### "Slam Dunk" Intangible Benefits Delivered by SAP

*"Infrastructure* – SAP builds an infrastructure that is critical for supporting growth." Remember those CIOs' spaghetti charts that show just how hocked up your current architecture is; SAP's integrated architecture is a real improvement for most companies implementing SAP.

*"Integration* – SAP is a seamlessly integrated system; data are entered once; and authorized user access real-time, accurate data." Experience suggests most businesses should be (and quietly are) seriously embarrassed by the data on which they operate. The marked improvements in data quality that SAP forces is truly one of SAP's compelling gifts to your organization. AMR Research, a well-respected, independent expert in the SAP field, found that 70% of organizations implementing SAP claimed improved

data quality and visibility as the primary benefit of their SAP implementation (almost two times any benefit cited).

*"Standardization* – SAP ensures standardized data, standardized reporting, and standardized business process flows across the organization."* SAP creates one version of the truth, upsetting (usually) the spreadsheet games people use to advocate their agendas. But one version of the truth can be a two-edged sword – attractive to your shareholders, certainly, but very challenging to personal agendas. Standardized data and processes always butt heads with "the way we do things here." Standardization is most likely to be your executives' litmus test; will they force the standardization that SAP offers but your organization loathes, or will they compromise appeasing personal agenda while significantly, even mortally, diluting this potentially powerful benefit?

*"Information Flow and Work Flow* – SAP's automated workflows enhance process efficiencies and provide a clear and effective audit trail that enhance data integrity." Agreed. As explained in earlier editions of this book, "All businesses are compartmentalized to one degree or another. The notion of workflow, the procedural automation of a business process, erases the old notion of compartmentalization.

Compartmentalized business allows for successful surgery ("the marketing worked and orders are pouring in!") while allowing the patient to die ("the raw materials arrived too late and we couldn't manufacture in time so the order was cancelled). Workflow, on the other hand, assigns responsibility, oversight, and control through the entire business processes. Workflow is the primary source of the benefits you seek from SAP."

*"Scalability* – SAP's customers can be flexible to changes occurring due to growth and industry transformations." In our

view, scalability is one of SAP's chief gifts to your organization. But the word scalability undershoots this important benefit. It is not just that you can scale up, or grow your operations relatively quickly. It is more the case that SAP gives you wonderful options: the ability to extend your business processes into your customers' operations, the capacity to quickly integrate acquisitions (at least from the process perspective), the capacity for creating and hiving off new operations. Business opportunities and threats morph daily; organizations that lack SAP's option value will find themselves increasingly lost in the dust.

### "Maybe" Intangible Benefits Promised by SAP

*"Improved Reporting* – SAP delivers accurate, accessible, and timely reports to end users at all level. End users have tools to create their own queries to capture data that are pertinent to them." First, define "improved." In the past, many business users of SAP were sorely disappointed with SAP's reports. It is not that SAP-generated reports were bad—for heaven's sake, it was the first time many organizations viewed *true* reports—they just weren't the customized reports people had grown to expect. Most SAP implementations now include a data warehouse capable of providing richer, more flexible reporting. In sum SAP delivers truer reporting, certainly. Better reporting, though, remains in the eye of the beholder.

*"Regulatory Compliance* – Updating Human Resource and payroll government regulations and guidelines is easy and clear with SAP; effective audit trails enhance data quality." This is a no-brainer benefit in heavily regulated industries, like pharmaceuticals or medical devices, or in heavily regulated parts of your business (think Finance under the reign of Sarbanes-Oxley, a set of regulations that make top executives personally responsible for financial controls and public reporting). SAP makes regulatory compliance a snap. But I've included this benefit in the Maybe

category because regulatory compliance is not always a burning issue for many businesses.

*"High Value Activities* – SAP allows personnel to devote more time to higher value activities." SAP has yet to prove the antidote to the silliness, pettiness, and inertia that ensures you spend too much time on non-value added work. Non-value added work CAN stop because of SAP, but it won't stop by itself. You have to deliberately re-engineer work whilst implementing SAP.

Remember: SAP may automate work and enhance your opportunities to focus on higher value added work, but it has yet to eliminate that waste-of-time Monday morning staff meeting.

## And in the End...

We have no doubt you will gain hard-dollar benefits from your SAP investments. We're confident you will receive multiple intangible benefits from your SAP investments.

But keep in mind the line from the Beatles song "The End" when you are planning your SAP investments. "And, in the end, the love you take is equal to the love you make." The benefits you will receive will reflect the thought and insight you bring to your SAP initiatives. Do you truly understand how your operations can improve? Do you equally understand how SAP's functionality can specifically help you work better, faster, and cheaper?

Do you have the courage and ability to do it right, to not rush toward your Go-Live date, tossing functionality – and benefits – overboard like your ship is sinking fast? Can you create a realistic business case for your SAP investment? Can you develop Key Performance Indicators that effectively measure and guide benefits delivery? Most importantly, can you convince the business to reflect your business case in their budgets and operating plans?

As a final thought, note that at no time did I use the dreaded "R" word in this chapter. There was a point when SAP and Re-engineering were intimately related. Michael Hammer, co-founder of last decade's "Re-engineering Revolution," produced an SAP video that was *de rigueur* for executives implementing SAP and did the star-turn at numerous SAP events. But it all seems very distant now. Re-engineering concepts, like lean operations and improving cycle time, still apply to most SAP implementations. But growing adherence to SAP's ASAP methodology, or some variation of it, led people away from re-engineering methods, like the creation of extensive AS-IS documentation, and toward ERP methods. And re-engineering's reputation suffered just as the SAP train was gaining its steam.

For most of us, we're using SAP's functionality to do business better, faster, and cheaper.

For those organizations where the re-engineering revolution is alive and well, by all means wrap your SAP initiative in re-engineering's overalls.

In truth, we do not care how you position your SAP implementation as long as you do those things that secure SAP's benefits.

As we advised in earlier editions of this book: "Call it re-decorating or re-engineering; just do it."

CHAPTER 8

# Enlightened Selection and Management of SAP Consultants

- ❏ The Frenzy is Over
- ❏ Global Delivery Models
- ❏ SAP Consulting Rates: What to Expect
- ❏ What SAP Consultants Do
- ❏ Choosing Your SAP Consultants Wisely
- ❏ Successful Partnerships with SAP Consultants

# Enlightened Selection and Management of SAP Consultants

## The Frenzy is Over

During SAP's frenzied growth from 1993-2000, SAP consulting was fairly immature. As previously mentioned, there were insufficient delivery methods until at least 1997 and the demand for SAP consultants far exceeded the supply.

Consider the story of a West Coast SAP haves-and-needs body-shopper that I often referred to as The Man Who Never Stops Laughing. In 1995, he was an executive search specialist, but he finally switched over to the placement of SAP contract consultants. His overhead consisted of an office, a computer, a website, and some very high phone bills. Whenever I called him, he giggled over his good fortune and, because he thought of me as an SAP prognosticator, he always, "How long will this SAP thing last?"

In those years, contract consultants wanted $125 to $200 an hour and this gentleman's take for finding them clients was $15-$30 for each hour that they billed. With anywhere from twenty to forty people working for him at a time, his income was around $600 an hour.

The "SAP thing" he was referring to was the low supply and high demand for consultants. In 1996, I assured him that he had at least three more years. Later, I tacked on another year or two. My first guess was right. My friend's SAP laughter came to a close in late 1999. Last I heard, he was brokering consultants in supply chain management.

From 1992 to the end of 1996, the failures of SAP consulting were considerable. R/3 was too new and few people knew how it worked, yet waves of inexperienced consultants debarked at Fortune 500 clients and earned their bones in a trial-by-error fashion. Implementation methods for traditional IT acquisition and development projects were applied to implementations, usually with costly results. The notion of business process re-engineering was also new and workflow was barely discussed.

As for the consultants themselves, there was a high level of unreliability (faked résumés, high attrition rates) as well as a high level of *prima donna* behavior. I could recount dozens of examples of SAP consultant weirdness, from the consultant who specified the minimum acceptable hotel room size and maximum distance from the client site to the consultant who worked for six firms in the space of one year, including three at the same time. This story, I believe, sums things up nicely: a consultant who worked in my practice in 1996, when asked to be at a client meeting on a given Friday, replied, "I do not fly on Thursdays."

Beginning in 1997, we could see a maturing at three levels of the SAP world. First, clients began to appreciate the differences between SAP and what they knew before it. Second, SAP America pitched in by hiring and training hundreds of consultants and by forming the Team SAP concept. Finally, the quality of SAP consulting improved through a combination of experience (those people who were rookies in 1993 now possessed four years of SAP experience) and method. The attraction of European consultants has long since faded as North American SAP expertise is now ubiquitous and none of the consultants I've met in recent years has an aversion to flying on Thursdays.

## Global Delivery Models

In the late 1990's, emerging India-based firms such as Tata Consultancy Services (TCS), Wipro, and Infosys began to subcontract with multinationals such as PwC Consulting (since merged into IBM GBS) and Accenture to provide peripheral technical services in the course of SAP engagements. These services included ABAP programming for customizations, report writing, data migration, and a host of other tasks that did not require onsite consultants. Because the costs of Indian labor are far less than North American labor, systems integrators were able to reduce blended rates from previous levels of $200+ per hour to under $200.

In more recent years, the deployment of a global delivery model has proliferated to the point at which the aforementioned India-based firms are now priming SAP contracts and every multi-national service provider has hundreds to thousands of SAP staff in India, China, Eastern Europe, Ireland, the Philippines, and elsewhere. Other India-based firms have also joined the fray, most notably Cognizant and Satyam, and even a number of second-tier firms such as Intelligroup have considerable SAP global resource.

At the same time, the level of sophistication of remote services provided has risen and now it is not at all uncommon to deploy global resources for software configuration in addition to the more peripheral tasks.

The result is that upwards of 50% of the SAP labor required for an engagement will be delivered from a remote location. While 50% has been deemed by most responsible SAP systems integrators as excessive and even dangerous, the effect on costs, even at lesser percentages of global involvement, has been impressive year over year, even as global rates are on the rise.

While there are many variations to the SAP global delivery model, here is a simple example of the model when applied to the configuration phase.

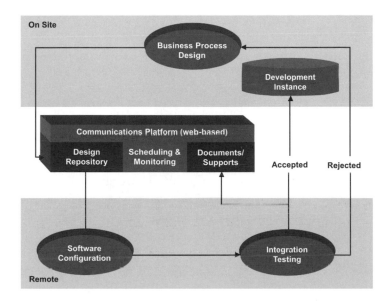

At the center of this model is a web-based communications platform that contains the design repository, resource scheduling and monitoring, and all documents and supports shared between on-site and remote resource.

This model allows the on-site team to concentrate on business process design and design objects are loaded to the design repository. Based upon these designs, software configuration and integration testing are done remotely (at less cost). Successful integration results in the configuration being loaded to the SAP development instance. Unsuccessful integration results require another round of process design.

Beyond cost containment, the global delivery model provides another big advantage: time compression. If the remote team is in a far different time zone (> 6-hour differential), the team can adopt what is called "follow the sun" by which, at the end of a day, the on-site team delivers process design to the remote team and at the beginning of the next day already has configuration results.

In essence, the project team is working on two shifts, thus vastly reducing delivery time.

The gains of a global delivery model are somewhat offset by added complexity. Here are some key elements to address when a global model is adopted.

❑ Knowledge transfer, especially in regard to software configuration, is essential so clients can maintain their configuration after the Go-Live date. This method sabotages any chance the client will have to gain this knowledge through participation in the configuration phase, so an alternate means of knowledge transfer must be sought. Clients are advised to re-invest some of the cost savings in additional knowledge transfer (unless, post-implementation, the applications will be outsourced).

❑ Because configuration is an iterative process, functional testing and horizontal integration testing may best be accomplished by on-site staff.

❑ Management of remote configuration is more complex than management of remote coding services. Remote staff may well not have the requisite business knowledge, product knowledge, and/or full understanding of horizontal business processes. If remote configuration teams lack this local leadership, configuration efforts will be more iterative than otherwise, thus eroding savings. Communications platforms can fill only a part of the gap.

## SAP Consulting Rates: What to Expect

We have kept a benchmark of these rates since 2001 that indicates that average blended rates have fallen from $180 per hour to a 2006 level of $155 per hour.

| Blended Rates | | From 2001 | From 2006 |
|---|---|---|---|
| 2001 | $180 | | |
| 2002 | $175 | 97% | |
| 2003 | $170 | 94% | |
| 2004 | $165 | 92% | |
| 2005 | $160 | 89% | |
| 2006 | $155 | 86% | |
| 2007 | $153 | | 99% |
| 2008 | $154 | | 99% |
| 2009 | $155 | | 100% |

Note that these rates apply for leading SAP systems integrators (Accenture, BearingPoint, Deloitte, et al) and are generally $15 to $20 less for systems integrators operating in the small & medium enterprise markets. When offshore resource is not included (i.e. when all resource is domestic), the average blended rate will be closer to $175.

India remains by far the predominant source of global SAP resource. None of the other geographies mentioned can match its combination of English-based IT education and massive population. While growth has been explosive, we are now seeing higher levels of attrition as the multi-national firms are successfully competing with India-based firms for Indian resource. The net effect is a rise of Indian rates and, by extension, a similar rate hike in other geographies.

Secondly, SAP's technical migration toward NetWeaver is in progress while the SAP client-base has begun to reflect acceptance of the new technology. While we will not be facing a shortage of experienced consultants as we did in the 1990's, there will be a clamor for rare NetWeaver skills in 2007-09, which will also have an effect on rates.

Following is a more granular composition of rate averages in 2007.

| Level | Top Tier Large Market | | | Second Tier SME | | |
|---|---|---|---|---|---|---|
| | High | Medium | Low | High | Medium | Low |
| Senior | $250 | $225 | $200 | $225 | $180 | $160 |
| Consulting | $200 | $180 | $175 | $175 | $150 | $125 |
| Remote | $60 | $45 | $35 | $60 | $45 | $35 |
| Average | $170 | $150 | $137 | $153 | $125 | $107 |

**Indy, They've Taken the Children From the Village!**

A number of SAP consulting firms offer 'ABAP factory' supports, usually overseas. Their lure is cheap ABAP customization and the shine to that lure is usually in the form of easy transmission of specifications from your site to the 'factory' and back. Treat such firms as you would treat the plague. Heavy customization of SAP will chain you to these firms forever. You will not be able to upgrade to newer SAP offerings without also updating all of the keen modifications that these firms will have made for you. In essence, such customization turns configurable software into the same old program mode of traditional (read: old-fashioned) systems.

In short, global delivery models should follow consulting best practices. Mass customization is a worst practice that leads to SAParalysis.

## What SAP Consultants Do

In an ideal world, SAP consultants provide a transfer of their SAP knowledge to the client until that client is self-sufficient, and then they disappear.

At the opposite end of the spectrum, SAP consultants turn your company into a laboratory environment in which they impose their methods and their attitude and things just plain go south.

Between these two poles, there is a lot to work with but let's concentrate on the ideal in hopes of avoiding its opposite.

There are essentially three timeframes in which SAP consultants can be crucial to your success in implementing SAP:

During the **planning stage**, senior consultants provide guidance for budgeting, team formation, the establishment of realistic expectations, and the creation of a do-able project master plan. They establish a foundation of coherent terminology and help you to express the vision of the endeavor to the company body.

During the business **development stage**, module consultants provide a transfer of SAP knowledge to client staff and shorten the learning curve in regard to business process re-engineering and the subsequent software configuration needed to reflect that re-engineering.

During the **technical development stage**, middleware, network, and programming consultants provide services that support the frame of the business development. Many companies outsource such services, even after completion of core implementation.

Education embraces all three of these timeframes and is at the heart of correct employ of consultants. This subject will be covered in Chapter 6: "Learning to Swim in the SAP Waters."

If properly utilized, few consultants are still around when you throw the post-implementation party. Having provided a boost to your staff, an acceleration of events, and a meaningful transfer of SAP knowledge, they should have long since said their good-byes.

The accent must be on transfer of knowledge so that you can reduce your dependency upon consultants. For example, module configuration should be *guided* by consultants, not handed over to them lock, stock, and barrel; if so, you will not be in a position to modify configurations once the consultants are gone. Time and budget pressures often lead client staff to accelerate events by unleashing the consultants (leaving it to the experts) but the short-term gains will be paid for in the long term.

While the technical side of an SAP engagement is not unimportant, clients will be most affected by those consultants who are heavily involved in business process design, knowledge transfer, and organizational change management. In this light, cribbing directly from "The SAP Consultant Handbook" (Doane & Reed):

> "Babysitters are paid by the hour, just like consultants. Think about what kind of babysitters you had as a kid. One just sat in the front the TV and yelled at you to be quiet. Another made you popcorn and sat you in front of the TV while she chatted on the phone. Yet another made you popcorn, turned off the TV, and read a book to you. But the best one, *the best one*, taught you how to make popcorn, showed you how to turn off the TV, and then taught you to read your very favorite story.

With only SAP skills, a consultant is more like the babysitter who can make popcorn, dial a phone, and manipulate the remote control of a television.

When it comes to consultants, the best ones learn what story a client wants to learn and makes certain that, before the end of the project, the client knows how to read that story and live it out."

## Choosing Your SAP Consultants Wisely

By my observation, first as an SAP consulting practice leader and later as an industry analyst, few firms do an adequate job of selecting their SAP systems integration partner. While at META Group, I had countless one-hour teleconferences with client firms that had already completed their short list. Few were able to provide a solid justification for the firms that they had settled upon. Many had an odd mix of "usual suspects" such as Deloitte and Accenture as well as a boutique outfit and an Indian-based firm just to "round things out." Too often it was apples to pineapples as the boutique firms responded with low cost bids but insufficient resource and scope of services.

Enlightened selection of an SAP systems integrator can bring immeasurable benefit to a firm. While the selection of the right systems integrator is of major import, so are the terms and foundation on which the engagement is made. Oftentimes, the "right" systems integrator is chosen for the wrong reasons and client expectations are not met. Equally as often, a systems integrator appears to be chosen for the right reasons but the selection process is flawed and client expectations are misplaced.

In addition, the selection process can be bewildering. Consulting skills, SAP skills, industry focus, methods & tools, organizational change management, knowledge transfer, and a host of other elements of an engagement all require scrutiny and clients are faced with a need to identify competitive advantages and disadvantages within the context of their specific needs and goals.

A brief definition of the "right" SAP systems integrator, derived from a combination of field experience and client input, is a firm that will embrace and enhance a client vision and bring measurable business benefit in an engagement that will also fully prepare the client to efficiently maintain and enhance its SAP assets well after the engagement is completed. While the adherence to time and cost is important, our experience and research strongly suggest that, over the long haul, these elements are less important than most clients believe. Deadlines are often capricious and cost is only half of the ROI equation.

It is recommended that clients follow a formal Request for Proposal (RFP) process preceded by enlightened shortlisting. To provide such enlightenment, clients can obtain SAP systems integrator buyer's guides from Performance Monitor in order to have more to go on than systems integrator's branding, value propositions, and reference clients. The complete recommended steps for a formal selection are outlined below:

1. **Establish Short-listing & Selection Criteria**

   Prior to short-listing, determine the attributes of the ideal service provider for your engagement. Is knowledge of your industry a must or is it only desirable? How important is knowledge transfer and client ownership of the engagement? Are you seeking creative financing or will you depend on fixed cost?

2. **Informed Short Listing**

   At least three candidate firms likely to match your criteria should be included on a short list. For large engagements, five candidate firms are recommended, with the notion that, at the point of written response to RFP, the two outliers will be immediately cast aside. Thus, clients have only three responses to the RFP to be assessed.

3. **Develop the RFP According to What You Want and Demand Response in the Form of the RFP**

   Clients often build an RFP with an eye on what they believe the service providers can do. Our advice to clients is to include precisely what is desired and leave it up to the candidate firms to best describe how they will satisfy the demand.

Most IT service providers have automated or semi-automated methods for responding to an RFP. If clients accept such responses, the diversity of response results in a great burden of extrapolation, cut & paste, and document backtracking. We have seen instances in which one vendor tendered a 325 screen PowerPoint, another sent four Word files and two Excel tables, and the other three sent boilerplate Word files. Service providers should be encouraged to include salient information in addendum to the RFP response.

We recommend advising all short-listed firms that a failure to respond to the form of the RFP may result in elimination.

## 4. Provide Sufficient Time for Response

For most engagements, candidate firms should have 3 to 4 weeks after their acknowledgement of receipt of the RFP. Clients should make every effort to deliver the RFP to a vendor contact who is capable of routing the RFP to the proper individual or entity for response. Firms that are not given sufficient time tend to return responses that a) are insufficiently competitive and/or b) do not adequately address RFP aims. The following is a representative timeline for the Request for Proposal Process.

| Week | Step | Comments |
|---|---|---|
| Week 0 | Distribute RFP | |
| Week 3 | Receive RFP Written Response | Add 1-2 weeks for very large-scale engagements |
| Week 4 | Response Assessment & Initial Scoring | Presumes responses are in the form of the RFP |
| Week 5 | 3 Finalist Presentations | Full day presentations for very large-scale engagement |
| Week 6 | Update Scoring | |
| Week 7 | Final Selection & Due Diligence | |

## 5. Establish and Maintain a Level Playing Field

The goal is to receive the most competitive responses possible. If any of the candidate firms presumes a client bias toward one of the firms on the list, the response will not be competitive and the purpose of the RFP process will be undermined.

## 6. Score Responses According to Weighted Criteria

Group scoring reduces the fog of vendor posturing, claims, lunches, peripheral phone calls, and the like. Scoring must be held against weighted criteria or results will be distorted.

## 7. Seek Out Differentiation While Flattening Price Points

If all responses are in the form of a client RFP, vendor differentiation is easy to identify and clients can immediately concentrate on points of contrast. If proposed costs are not widely diverse, clients can encourage higher-priced vendors to re-structure their response to meet the lowest current bid. This is the advantage of being in a buyers' market.

## 8. Observe Vendor Behavior Throughout the Process

Vendor behavior and tactics through the RFP process reveal the passion or lack thereof that a vendor has for the client's engagement. Clients should note whether vendors respond on a timely basis, are readily available to answers questions regarding the response, and assign the right resource to the task at hand.

During vendor presentations, clients should take note of who presents. Presentations by prospective project managers and support staff provide a client the opportunity to assess how that firm might actually perform. Presentations led by sales directors, partners, or senior managers reveal less.

Clients should penalize attempts by vendors to seek outside leverage on decision-makers through contact with parties not included on the evaluation and decision-making committee such as board members, peer groups or other client associates. Client should also penalize attempts by vendors to discredit client evaluation team members (and/ or third party influencers) who do not seem inclined to choose them.

## 9. Cost is Its Own Criteria

When making a final selection of an IT service provider, clients should balance final scoring against proposed cost. If one vendor has a large scoring lead but is marginally more costly than the second place vendor, clients should determine whether the differential in capability is worth the difference in cost.

Finally, clients should be looking for a vendor's demonstrable ability to provide measurable business benefits as a result of any engagement. Time & cost alone are no longer the key criteria for SAP project success.

Further, since every candidate firm will claim a desire to be your partner, keep an eye out for evidence behind this claim. If all they are doing is working on your project and billing you for it, they can hardly be viewed as a partner. If, however, their offer is sweetened by a high level of risk/reward or the bestowal of "premier client" status by which special terms or services are provided, some semblance of partnership may be in the offing.

It is important to remember that each of the firms you consider will have a distinctly different culture. We have learned this not only from close observation of the leading SAP systems integrators but also through the research results. In parallel to assessing a vendor's capabilities, client organizations will seek a cultural fit and this leads to more subjective, and still valid, results.

In the final analysis, enlightened selection of an SAP systems integrator will be based upon the right combination of demonstrable capabilities (criteria results), cost, and culture.

## Successful Partnerships with SAP Consultants

Once a client has chosen an SAP systems integrator, a partnership commences in which both parties should be counted on to pull their weight.

As evidenced in "SAP by the Numbers," however, partnership tends to falter right out of the gate as clients turn an ungainly amount of attention to the adherence to time and budget at the cost of gaining business benefit.

The best practices for successfully partnering with an SAP systems integrator are:

1.  Take a high level view of client ownership. This means getting down deep into understanding and adhering to the delivery methodology and tools, accelerating your SAP knowledge transfer, and participating not only in business process design but also in software configuration.

    If you "leave it to the experts" your costs will rise, you will fail to gather skills needed to thrive after Go-Live, and the results may not be what you were expecting.

2.  Establish measurable goals. This advice is repeated at least fifty times in this book for good reason. With measurable goals, you and your systems integrator have a common destination toward which you can road map. If the only destination is a deadline, and even if you make that deadline, you will fail.

3.  Listen carefully to your consulting leadership and do not seek to tweak or tinker the methodology in an attempt to "cut to the chase."

4. Place a high priority on post-implementation concerns even at the sacrifice of budget and time adherence. Focus on long-term concerns, not the short-term.

This last point is difficult for project sponsors and managers to accept as they are probably being judged by their organization on a basis of time and cost adherence. The fact is, if you do run late and over budget, the saving grace will be an ability to point out measurable business gains that will make the cost and time overruns pale in comparison.

# CHAPTER 9

# Learning to Swim in the SAP Sea

# Learning to Swim in the SAP Sea

## Swimming Lessons or Lifeboats

You were thinking of skipping this chapter or, at best, skimming it. Already your fingers were reaching to page ahead to something more "compelling."

The remainder of this book loses its useful luster if SAP education is swept under the rug. Consider this: would you invest $100,000 in a Lamborghini and then entrust it to someone without a driver's license? This is just what many firms have done by making a multi-million-dollar investment in SAP software and consulting while providing relative crumbs for associated education. Later, when their Lamborghini fails to reach high speed or, worse, crashes into the garage door, it is usually the consultants, those easy targets, who are given the blame.

Moreover, most firms base their training budgets and scenarios on the 'last war' basis, still thinking of the training that was provided for systems that preceded SAP. That is to say, they think only of end user training and neglect the other necessary waves of education. By the same token, most training is geared to the latter stages of an implementation project, but a more effective schedule calls for layered phases of training/ education according to the evolution of the project.

| Level | SAP | Change Mgmt | When |
|---|---|---|---|
| Executive | Understand the new enterprise | Develop the vision | Acquisition |
| | | Share the vision | Planning stage |
| Middle Mgmt | Continuous re-engineering | How to exploit MIS | Planning stage |
| Supervisors | How to seize benefits-workflow | Supervise change | Development stage |
| | | Form new career paths | |
| Project Team | Module training | Consulting skills | Planning stage |
| | Integration/team training | | |
| Direct Users | Module trainings | Business perspective | Implementation stage |
| | Integration | New career path | |

## Executives Are Seldom Taught but They Can Learn

Since early 1996, I have provided an SAP executive seminar that ranges in length from half a day to two days. The subjects largely cover those that are included in this book but the sessions are tailored to audience size, nature, and need. When this seminar was first conceived, it was assumed that it would be sought by firms that were considering SAP and so felt a need to learn more about it.

A high percentage of companies that sign up for the seminar are those that have already endeavored to implement SAP and are finding that a major hurdle is the ignorance of their own management. Either the project is being stalled because of management misunderstanding of the venture or the project is succeeding at the implementation level but management is in the dark about what is taking place. When senior management acquires SAP and then leaves it to the experts to "put it in," the result is seldom pretty.

It is highly recommended that senior management be roped into a useful seminar at the beginning of the project, but if this cannot be arranged, a seminar or course should be made available to these people just as the core implementation is coming to a close. This after-the-fact education will be like offering a surprise to those people who would, ideally, have been supporting you all along. The reality is, they probably will not have much idea what it is the project team has been up to.

The thrust and content of senior management education should be:

❑ an exposition of the historical and business context of SAP

❑ a revelation of the critical differences between SAP and traditional systems and the consequent impact on their organizations

❑ the benefits of workflow as the heart of the matter

❑ the import and content of change management and a delineation of their role in this context.

It is probable that the greatest impediment to such education will be the unwillingness of senior management to invest the time for it. Senior management usually wants 'nugget' information, summary data, or overviews, and will wrongly assume that 'management education to SAP' is going to consist of a detailed technical presentation concerning software. Coaxing senior managers to learn something is a tough task, but it can be made easier if the lead subject of the seminar (do not call it a course; senior managers do not attend 'courses') is something other than 'SAP.' Call it a "Seminar on the New State of Absolutely Everything in this Company" and you might get a positive RSVP.

## Education for Middle Management

Middle management is usually comprised of individuals whose patience with an SAP implementation will be the most tested. It is they who are keeping an eye on the budget and timescale and it is on their desks that complaints and conflicts will land. In most instances, it is also this group that has the distinct notion that the implementation will have a visible endpoint and will, in essence, be over.

The education required for this group addresses two timeframes of effort: during implementation and after implementation.

The content of education for middle management should include much of the same as for senior management, while offering more detail in terms of:

❑ the intricacies and benefits of workflow

❑ the concept of continuous re-engineering

❑ implementation blueprints

❑ case study laboratory

Supervisors fall under the same category for education, whether they participate in the seminars with middle management or are trained separately.

## Project Team Training

Rigorous, multi-level education of your SAP Project Team is an investment that leads to continual returns. If this training is properly completed, your firm will not only be in a position to effectively implement SAP, but also to seize SAP benefits on an ongoing basis.

The benefits of team training, in addition to SAP module training, are numerous:

1. A reduction of configuration time due to a heightened awareness of integration points within SAP and a greater awareness of individual roles and responsibilities.

2. A reduction of customization or modifications due to improved internal consulting skills

3. The establishment of an accent on benefits and return-on-investment.

4. The formation of a team mentality prior to field work, which reduces trial-and-error.

5. The probable retention of project staff after the core implementation is completed.

### Phase 1: Take it from the Top

The business basics of SAP should be established at the very beginning. The project team should be given the same seminar that is offered to senior and middle management. Module-specific training that follows will be of great use for the daily nuts and bolts of implementation, but unless a distinctly identifiable business environment is established, the subsequent configuration exercise may drift.

The SAP implementation team overview should focus on:

- the intricacies of workflow

- implementation blueprints

- case study laboratory

- the pitfalls of an SAP implementation

- the business process re-engineering/configuration iterative loop.

## Phase 2: Seeing with a Horizontal View

Configuration skills are not limited to individual modules because of the high degree of integration that is the core of SAP. Thus, prior to SAP level 2 and 3 module training, team members should receive a course in integration and configuration.

Some courses exist that last two weeks and provide an instructor-guided microcosm of an SAP implementation at the level of configuration and integration.

An education experience such as a learning environment configuration and testing of a system will be the most useful activity at this point. Giving your team members a hands-on experience with the core modules FI, SD, MM, PP will provide far more benefit than would lecture or reading.

## Phase 3: The Vertical View

Depending on assigned roles, various team members will be schooled in specific areas such as FI, SD, MM, or PP. Such training usually includes two levels, the first of which is module overview and the second is module mastery. Configuring SAP's individual modules is at the heart of this training and it should be noted that training alone will not always suffice to prepare an individual for the demands of a project. There is no substitute for configuring experience.

## Phase 4: Field Guidance

This last phase of training, which generally lasts about five days, prepares your team in the areas of realistic project and phase planning, scope management, consulting skills, and the application of sound methodology. Without this training, you will have a cadre of SAP-savvy employees who will nevertheless be unprepared for the smell of configuring gunpowder, the rattling of consultant sabers, the trumpet blasts of user meetings, or the lightning fires of scope changes; in short, all that will occur in the project that does not directly address the product.

Consulting skills should not be neglected; without them, your SAP project team member may fail. A case in point: a European SAP consultant I once knew had more than five years of experience in FI. At a key point in a project, he found himself unable to convince client staff why certain steps had to be taken for their system to work the way they wanted. His tactic with the client was to pound the table and tell them that he knew SAP and they did not, so they should take his word as Bible. This is the case of a team member who had sufficient training in levels 1 through 3 but clearly insufficient training for the all-important level 4.

At the conclusion of these four levels of training, you will have a project team that is ready for a final test.

## Phase 5: Field Testing the Project Team

Team training for SAP implementation groups is a fairly new concept that is gaining currency because of the success that many firms have had. Team members will have to present themselves as consultants as well as SAP specialists and they will have to work as an integrated team because of the highly integrated nature of

SAP. Without team training, you will have a cluster of module specialists, all knowledgeable in their own subjects but largely ignorant of the fully horizontal picture.

What we recommend is a final consequential training phase in which your team members be assembled for a two-week team training exercise during which their team and SAP skills will be tested and refined in parallel.

Each member will assume a role similar to that which is planned for your firm. Teams will be comprised of at least one person each for FI, SD, MM, and PP (and, optionally) HR, with one person chosen as project manager. During the first three days of the course, attendees will be presented with a detailed case study. During the remaining seven days, each team will strive to satisfy the business case by configuring SAP. During these seven days, instructors fill the role of "enlightened" clients, offering guidance in terms of the business case but not detailed instruction as in phase 2. At the same time, your team members will be evaluated in terms of consulting skills, team skills, and SAP implementation and configuration skills.

## End User Training

This training, which ideally will occur just before SAP is put into play, can be accomplished in a variety of ways, including:

**Super User Model,** in which designated users are fully trained by the project team members and then pass on that training to their cohorts.

**Project Team,** in which module specialists are responsible for the training of their relevant user groups.

**Outsourced Training,** in which end user training specialists use project documentation as a basis for training of user groups.

There are no absolute methods that must be followed for end user training. These methods are often mixed to the advantage of a project. For example, outsourcing is chosen but project team members are also involved as is a super user so that project team members provide SAP context, super users provide end business use context and credibility, and the outsourcing specialist provides techniques and experience for the creation of training materials.

| Method | Advantage | Disadvantage |
|---|---|---|
| Super User | The user group takes responsibility for making it all work | Hard to ID a super user; super users do not always know the answer to 'Why?' |
| Project Team | Can answer the question 'Why?' | Not empathetic to user group concerns; maintains responsibility at project team level |
| Outsource | Training specialists are on the scene | Lack of project context |

Note that the standard method for creating core end user training materials is to take key documents created in the TO BE phase, such as process scripts and convert them from specifications to guides.

Whatever methods are chosen to accomplish end user training, these are the two best practices:

1. Do not shortchange initial end user training. Since it usually occurs as the penultimate step before Go-Live, many firms, running late and over-budget, cut corners in this regard.

2. Train your end users within the context of their business processes. If they are simply provided functional training (how to enter a sales order, how to update a financial transaction), they will be deprived of an understanding of their role in the flow of business. This will seriously impede their ability to seize the intended benefits.

3. Establish continuous training, including the necessary resource, budget, and authority.

While points 1 and 2 are of major import, point 2 is essential. Prior to implementing SAP, clients replaced individual applications (sales order processing, accounting, purchase order processing) every three to four years and in the course of these replacements, users received new training. Your SAP installation is going to last twenty to thirty years; your user base cannot wait that long for its next round of training.

Further to this point, attrition alone should drive firms to provide continuous training. According to input from the Bureau of National Affairs, the recent average attrition rate for positions comparable to those occupied by SAP end users is 12.4%.

| 12.40% Attrition Rate | | | | | | | |
|---|---|---|---|---|---|---|---|
| 0 | Attrition | End Yr 1 | Attrition | End Yr 2 | Attrition | End Yr 3 |
| 1000 | 124 | 876 | 109 | 767 | 95 | 672 |
| | | 124 | | 233 | | 328 |
| | | 12.40% | | 23.30% | | 32.80% |

Note: Attrition rates are generally higher for sub-managerial positions such as those occupied by end-users.

The table above shows that if you have 1,000 users on the day of Go-Live and follows this same attrition pattern, within three years you will have lost a third of your base.

If you adopt a "user trains the user" approach, you are doomed to mediocrity as outgoing staff cannot be relied upon to provide replacement training.

Finally, your SAP installation is going to change. Whether it changes slowly or with great velocity, this is the scenario that will play out if you do not have a continuous training program.

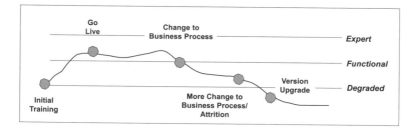

The following is an outline maturity model for SAP end user competency.

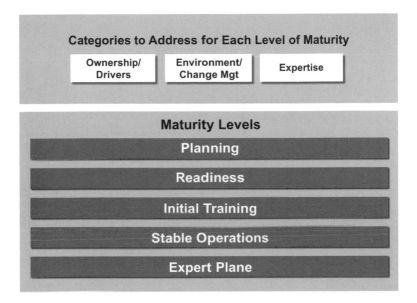

One of the greatest impediments toward fulfilling this maturity model is the question of "ownership of SAP competency." Is it the realm of HR, of IT, of business? In 2003, I put out a survey with the question: "Who in your organization is responsible for SAP competency?" The most frequent responses among 112 respondents were "do not know" and "no one."

## Racing to the Expert Plane

Early, hands-on SAP education addresses the following characteristics of SAP projects:

❑ The learning curve for your internal project team.

❑ Organizational change may lead to employee resistance.

❑ The element of an enterprise-wide implementation means that planning will encompass the entire enterprise.

You must prepare for resistance, and plan on the time it takes to smooth it over. You must also be prepared for a steep learning curve, not only for your project staff but also for every employee affected by the project. Here is the kind of progress you might expect.

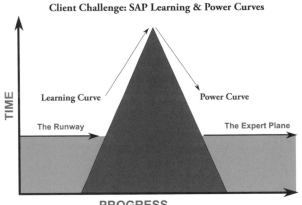

Client Challenge: SAP Learning & Power Curves

The speed with which a client reaches the Expert Plane has a direct correlation with the indirect (or variable) costs of the core implementation. Consulting costs rise in direct proportion to the scale of the learning and power curves.

**The Runway:** The earliest phases of a project are a time during which you develop the vision, form a team, create a budget and master plan, send a few key players off to SAP training courses and prepare for the main body of the project.

During the runway phase, only the immediate project team and some members of upper management are directly affected, and the balance of the company populace is still out of the loop.

**The Learning Curve:** Once configuration begins, the learning curve grows steep and daunting. What seemed, during the planning phases, like a row of hills, is revealed to be a full-scale mountain range.

Increasingly, client staff begins to grasp the complexity and the power of SAP. Project teams are tempted to expand project scope to take ever more advantage of potential benefits.

How to shorten the learning curve? Plan on it in advance, and make sure that the consulting role includes energetic transfer of knowledge. Further, client staff should be given early product and integration training, and management should become educated about SAP, what it is for, what it can do, and how it differs from classical systems implementation projects. Such education should occur during the project preparation phase and well before realization begins in earnest.

**The Power Curve:** Once you have begun to scale the learning curve, the power curve will begin as well. Where these curves cross may decide the fate of your project and will certainly affect project costs.

The power curve is revealed in the time it takes for your firm to make decisions relative to the business processes to be adopted as part of the SAP implementation. If there has been knowledgeable management commitment from the outset, this curve is shortened.

The duration of this curve is determined by the levels of unity, management, and communications of a firm, as well as by the quality of preparation during the runway phase.

The power curve ends when there is a general consensus that SAP is still going to be implemented according to a defined vision, and those who have ridden the learning curve will lead that implementation.

**The Expert Plane:** Once the learning and power curves have been scaled, a firm can reach the expert plane. At this point, you will have taken ownership of the software and project and the outside consultants will no longer be driving progress.

The firms that gain the most benefit from an SAP implementation are those that have reached the expert plane and continue to seek new benefit from the installed base. Such firms maintain an SAP implementation group in a continuous business improvement environment.

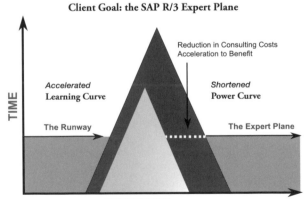

Client Goal: the SAP R/3 Expert Plane

# CHAPTER 10

# Hearts, Minds, Pink Slips, & Career Paths
*by Michael Connor*

❑ Taking The Plunge

❑ Change Management Element #1
Program Governance

❑ Change Management Element #2
Risk/Readiness Assessment

❑ Change Management Element #3
A Leadership Program

❑ Change Management Element #4
A Communications Program

❑ Change Management Element #5
A Job Alignment Approach

❑ Change Management Element #6
A PowerUser Program

❑ Change Management Element #7
A Knowledge Transfer Process

❑ Change Management Element #8
Role Based Training

# Hearts, Minds, Pink Slips, & Career Paths

## Taking the Plunge

Here's a quick joke. A CEO and her direct report walk into a bar. The direct report says, "I plan to spend 15% of our SAP budget on Change Management and Training." "You do that and you will be looking for a new job," the CEO replies. "Do it as cheaply as possible."

Wait, that's not a joke. It is the sad reality surrounding most SAP implementations.

Change Management comprises all actions taken to hasten receipt of benefits from your SAP investments.

Change Management accomplishes this lucrative task by ensuring your organization uses SAP's functionality and your new, streamlined business processes to work better, faster, and cheaper.

We believe that most of the perceived failure around ERP in general is the result of insufficient or misguided Change Management efforts. Quite simply, the struggling organizations were not prepared to work in a new manner or, worse, were allowed to ignore SAP's new methods and practices.

We further believe that Change Management is an unwelcome step-child during many SAP implementations because people do not truly understand the problem that Change Management solves.

Let's be frank: an SAP implementation disrupts the cozy confines of "business as usual." As we wrote in earlier editions of this book, "As new business processes are contemplated, old jobs are placed into limbo, new jobs are ill-defined, turf is eliminated, habits are broken, traditions are trampled some people are absent and others have survival guilt, past skills are no longer honored, and training for necessary new skills is hard to find."

It is harsh but true: "Any project intended to be of benefit to the company may not be of benefit to each and every individual in that company. There will be losers, and they will not necessarily be of the 'dead wood' variety that needed to be swept away."

The problem that Change Management solves is the paradox we call Active Inertia. Sir Isaac Newton noted that bodies at rest tend to stay at rest. We further note that organizations who like where they are resting will actively go out of their way to stay at rest, including, if needed, acting indifferent to proposed changes, deploying passive aggressive resistance to leadership's agenda, dismissing your Program Manager's best attempts to deliver training, even sabotaging, if needed, small changes in daily policies and procedures (after all, the word sabotage came about when workers shoved their shoes called 'sabots', into machines as protest against mechanization).

The problem that Change Management solves, then, is the particularly virulent form of Active Inertia that SAP initiatives can engender.

First, consider the powerful emotions and concerns SAP programs typically arouse:

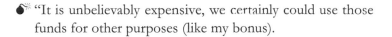

- 💣 "It is unbelievably expensive, we certainly could use those funds for other purposes (like my bonus).

- 💣 "It is a huge risk to business, I know someone who worked at a company that implemented SAP and they said it was painful to implement and lots of people lost their jobs."

- 💣 "Consultants have run amok, we're spending a fortune on a bunch of kids and honestly I can't help but believe management has lost faith in us."

- 💣 "SAP automates work, we'll need fewer people and I could lose my job."

- 💣 "It is an integrated system; to me that means everyone can see my mistakes, which means I could lose my job."

- 💣 "SAP robs me of the power I worked so hard to gain. I controlled what people did and what they knew, now a system will do this in spite of me."

Powerful emotions ignite powerful responses. Organizations that fear SAP fight SAP.

And too many organizations have proven successful resisting SAP's advances, rendering SAP a technical success but business failure. SAP "administers" the business, meaning data go in and reports come out, but it does not substantially change how the business operates; too much work is still accomplished outside the system, either in the form or user-exits from the system, workarounds that ignore system functionality, or work that was never automated in the first place.

An effective SAP Change Management solution makes peace before the SAP war can begin. It provides a credible rationale for change. It delivers the organizational and group support that gets an organization through a sustained period of uncertainty and disruption. It equips people to adopt new, better ways of work. And it proves that the uncertainty and tumult was worth it by demonstrating where, how, and to what extent you are gaining hard and strategic benefits from SAP.

As we wrote in earlier editions of this book, "Common wisdom says that people are naturally resistant to change. This is scarcely precise. People are naturally resistant to blind change or to change that is thrust upon them without explanation or justification."

So how can you ensure that SAP is not thrust upon your organization without explanation or justification? The answer to this question lies in how you design and deploy your SAP Change Management program.

A typical SAP Change Management program includes some sort of risk or readiness assessment, a set of leadership activities, a communications program, a PowerUser or SuperUser program, and a training program. This bare bones approach will work but misses important elements of a truly effective Change Management initiative.

An effective SAP Change Management initiative includes the above mentioned activities plus an overarching approach to program Governance; methods for aligning existing jobs with SAP-driven roles; tactics for supporting new, SAP-driven roles; and processes for measurably transferring critical knowledge from your implementation partner(s) to your implementation team and support organization(s).

Let's examine the rationale, design, and deployment of each element of an effective SAP Change Management program.

## Change Management Element #1: Program Governance

Program Governance assigns explicit roles and responsibilities to all parties involved in your SAP implementation. Designing governance processes deserves a book unto itself. According to SAP, major responsibilities to be addressed by Program Governance include:

**Business Authority:** Establish a Steering Committee that sets the business agenda and directs and empowers your design authority.

**Design Authority:** Task personnel to define, manage, and control how business critical elements such as best business practice, business process flows, and data standards are encapsulated in the SAP system, and how they are controlled across the SAP architecture.

**Build Responsibility:** These personnel take the design specifications and configure and test the SAP system to reflect defined business processes and data structures

**Roll-Out:** These personnel take the configured SAP system and implement the new business system into business organizational elements (division, region, line of business, etc.). Their tasks include data clean-up, user training, and managing the change program.

**Support:** These personnel provide post go-live support to your users and make ongoing changes and enhancements to the system. These changes may be minor functional changes or new reports. These personnel are usually part of a new organization called your 'SAP Competency Centre' or "SAP Center of Excellence."

**Maintenance:** These personnel provide the operational IT service and manage your server infrastructure, network, data management and disaster recovery.

These responsibilities are not mutually exclusive; in most cases select personnel will own multiple responsibilities. For example, design, build, and roll-out responsibilities are typically shouldered by your SAP Program Management Office. Support and Maintenance, on the other hands, are oftentimes split between an SAP Center of Excellence charged with supporting the company's SAP instance(s) while the existing IT organization addresses maintenance. In truth there is no one way to apportion responsibilities.

As a rough rule of thumb we believe your SAP Program Governance scheme is complete when you are confident you know who's responsible for making key decisions in each area, who's responsible for making sure the wrong things do not happen (like shortchanging testing), and who pays when the wrong things *do* happen (it's called accountability, and it's rarely popular).

## Change Management Element #2:
## Risk/Readiness Assessment

Remember, employees who disdain SAP will fight SAP. An effective Risk or Readiness Assessment should head off negative perceptions before the skirmishes begin.

There are literally thousands of ERP Readiness Assessments (an August 2007 Google search on "ERP Readiness Assessment" returns 23,800 hits). How best to choose?

All Risk/Readiness Assessments should measure the degree to which your organization is ready to support SAP's work changes, or conversely the degree to which your organization runs the risk of fighting SAP's changes. And since numbers are the language of business, it's far better to use a tool that delivers a numeric score (i.e. your risk score is -20) as opposed to some sort of qualitative or soft calibration (i.e. your organization is 'at risk').

An effective SAP Risk or Readiness Assessment must be actionable—the tool must specify how and why you need change your Planning, Implementation, Program Management, or Change Management approaches, and ideally it subsequently measures the efficacy of these changes through future measurements. Think of your Risk/Readiness Assessment as the hub or the centerpiece of your Change Management Program. Your first assessment describes the size and nature of your Change Management challenges. Subsequent assessments provide feedback on the efficacy of your Change Management efforts and provide fresh insights into your organization's evolving support for or resistance to your SAP efforts.

Let me provide an example. For the past decade we've used a Risk/Readiness Assessment during SAP implementations called the Readiness Quotient™ (RQ). RQ is grounded in the field of psychometrics, meaning it's based on solid science, and it's been deployed globally to over 20,000 people.

How does RQ work (or for that matter how should any effective SAP Risk/Readiness Assessment work)? RQ is administered to organizations implementing SAP. We typically engage a sample of end-user, project team members, and business sponsors in the RQ process.

RQ has two components: a data collection exercise and an Immersion, or root cause exercise. The data collection exercise is based around a conceptual model that describes what must happen for organizations to successfully adopt ERP. An Aside: There is no holy grail of conceptual models around change, despite what your friendly consultant is telling you. Just be sure there is a change model at the heart of your SAP Assessment and that the model makes sense to you and your business counterparts.

The RQ data collected during the data collection exercise are run through a piece of proprietary software that generates a single score measuring the degree to which the organization is supporting or fighting the SAP initiative. The software also identifies the specific perceptions that undermine support for your SAP initiative.

The Immersion exercise then drills into these negative perceptions (called Stumbling Blocks) to identify what's really going on, what it means for the success of your SAP initiative, and (most important) what can be done to address program risks.

What results from an RQ program is a numeric score, which proves very effective at communicating where you are on your SAP journey; insight into why you are in the position you are in; and actions, suggested by those impacted by the SAP program, as to what it will take for your program to succeed.

Consider one company who used RQ to guide their SAP initiative to success. Initial RQ scores looked rosy—the organization's leaders, program office, and end users all had phenomenal scores—but deeper examination of the RQ data pinpointed a latent risk. While people were eager to support their SAP initiative, few really understood where and how they could "plug into" the project. The frustrations suggested by comments like, "Why are our good intentions being ignored?" could have easily cascaded into widespread withdrawal from the SAP initiative. Instead, this client wisely amped up their Change Management program, creating multiple new opportunities for company personnel to participate and support the company's Blueprinting, Testing, Training, and Rollout Planning work streams.

RQ provides a dynamic measure of organizational readiness for SAP's changes. Organizations in the early throes of an SAP implementation are typically "frozen"—personnel haven't yet decided whether they are for or against their SAP initiative, but they are intrinsically cynical that SAP will deliver any benefit to them personally.

Organizations with good leadership and effective Change Management programs typically grow support by addressing individual cynicism, using communications, training, and on-the-job support to help end-users adopt new ways of work. RQ scores steadily improve in these organizations, providing solid proof that your Change Management investments are bearing fruit.

Organizations lacking leadership or effective Change Management typically overlook or try to overrun personal concerns, pushing SAP upon an unprepared and understandably hostile. RQ scores start neutral but then plunge as the initiative unfolds, providing a warning (we hope) that this implementation is headed for failure.

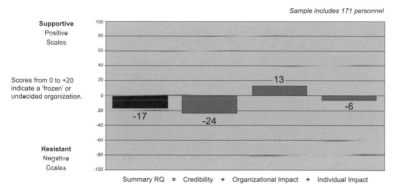

*Sample includes 171 personnel*

## Change Management Element #3:
## A Leadership Program

An effective SAP Leadership program is a marriage of style and substance.

Stylistically, we observe executives sponsoring or leading SAP programs must:

**Very Publicly Recognize Reality.** The ground is rapidly and scarily shifting under your organization's feet, and your people hope you can honestly and consistently recognize reality. "The scariest thing about this (SAP) implementation is how out of touch our sponsors are about what SAP will do to this organization," one Program Manager told me well into his troubled SAP program. Program and personal credibility hinge on your ability to consistently demonstrate you are in-touch with your organization's version of reality and willing and capable of making decisions and taking actions that are consistent with their interests.

**Very Credibly Show Respect.** SAP cannot succeed as something "done to us." People want to believe they are part of a larger whole and that it's not just about the executives at the top. All elements of your Leadership Program should conspire to the honestly communicate the "ups and downs," "hows and whys" of your SAP program. "I understand why we're going to SAP," one mid-level manager told me, "and I especially appreciate the opportunities our executives have created to hear from them and to voice our concerns"

**Very Quickly Take Action.** People want leaders who are taking them someplace worthy. They especially want to believe their leaders have real ability to get them there. "This (SAP) is doomed," one System Integrator commented over drinks. "I've never seen an organization so incapable of getting off the dime—they'll plan this thing for a year or two and then move on to the next great adventure" (which proved to be true in this case).

Grounded in reality, based on respect, prone to action: how can you design an SAP Leadership program that achieves these goals?

An SAP Leadership program has two objectives: ensure business leaders really lead your SAP implementation and credibly demonstrate the importance of your SAP initiative to your organization.

The worst leadership is all mouth. Effective SAP leaders are known for what they've done, not what they've said. You certainly aren't rolling up your sleeves and configuring the SAP software, but you are going to be called upon to make the decisions that determine how the software is configured. So "Issues Management"—the process of anticipating, presenting, and closing out the decisions your executive must make during your SAP initiative is an important part of your Leadership program.

Most Leadership programs favor mechanics over substance-- attend these meetings, talk to these people, have your elevator speech at the ready. Meetings can be important—of course, they can also be a bore, a waste of time, and a prime opportunity to diminish yourselves in the eyes of those you lead. To avoid these pitfalls we advise leaders implementing SAP to ensure there is real substance to every meeting—tell people something they do not know—and to listen, listen, and listen to those you are leading.

Much energy is expended creating the infamous "elevator speech"—the thirty second pitch every executive is schooled to deliver at the drop of a hat. There's undoubtedly value in refining the message, or simplifying the key messages that every executive should master. But we like to think of them as "elevator points," to be made informally, credibly, and only as circumstances allow.

Bottom line, do not be a bore, do not be a suit, do be informative, and be ALL about the actions and the outcomes.

As Michael Doane puts it, "Leadership alone will not sustain you. People come and go. Politics intervene. You have to create an atmosphere in which your employee body embraces change, the new responsibilities that come with that change, and the business capabilities that are derived from that change. If too much leadership is needed, success will be elusive."

## Change Management Element #4:
## A Communications Program

A workforce that is well informed and secure in its value to the company is less likely to question management and cause harm to the direction of your project. Conversely, we observe those organizations practicing "mushroom management"—keep everyone in the dark and heap manure on them—tend to fail miserably when implementing any ERP.

The overall goals of your SAP communications campaign is to gain employee engagement and support for your SAP initiative and to simultaneously reduce resistance to change. A two-pronged *push/pull* communications strategy achieves these goals.

**Push Marketing:** The objective of push marketing is to create awareness of and credibility for your SAP program. This communications strategy includes a visible marketing campaign with consistent key messages. Such communication includes general educational information such as a "what-why-how" overview for a high-level approach, as well as a description of the organizational/personal benefits to be gained through completion of the project. To improve credibility, the high-level messages should be communicated regularly by company leadership and coordinated with ongoing communications that are delivered by the management team.

**Pull Marketing:** The objective of pull marketing is to engage the employee population in such a fashion that they individually participate in the success of the change project. This strategy includes interactive communications that provide the opportunity for employees to actively understand and ultimately accept proposed work and policy change. So called Immersion Sessions, facilitated small group meetings, allow employees to voice their concerns about SAP's impacts and offer recommendations for increasing the program's chances for success.

In our experience eight factors will demonstrably affect the success of your SAP communications program.

**Leadership Support:** It is simple. If leadership does not believe in the impending changes and support the company's direction with visible action, employees will let their fear lead to resistance.

**Definition of Audience(s):** It is critical to have a clear understanding of your audience(s). At a minimum there will be variation between how messages are tailored and/or presented to leadership groups, management teams, and the general employee population. A further drill-down may lead to message segmentation by job type/experience level, employee location, implementation schedule, and other factors.

**Credible and Practical Messages:** Communications must make SAP's impacts "as real as possible, as fast as possible" to all levels of the organization. Communications must help people understand the group and personal impacts of SAP in a credible fashion, ensuring that people understand why at a gut level they should support the SAP initiative.

**Clear and Repetitive Messages:** Messages should be presented in a format that employees can review with ease. It is necessary to repeat the key messages on a regular basis. Employees must clearly understand the "what-why-how-when" behind the project in order to be comfortable with the changes it will bring.

**Confirmation of Communication Channels:** Your methods of communicating SAP's impacts may vary depending upon the audience. Face-to-face meetings can be the most direct approach, especially if the presenter is well-respected and credible. Other communication vehicles such as email, printed direct mail, advertising, posters/flyers, and/or promotional events work well in conjunction with direct management contact.

**Networks, Not Cascades:** Communications cascades are based on the notion that change messages work through the organization in a sequential, level-driven fashion (executive to manager to supervisor to individual contributors). In many of today's organizations, however, the hierarchy does not exist to make a communication cascade work. In that case communications should diffuse through the organization, leveraging the power of internal, informal networks and existing information flows to reinforce the credibility of key change messages.

**Customization:** Tailor the communications program as needed to ensure that it is effective and taken seriously. Broaden the reach or target the messages as appropriate.

**Closing the Loop:** Your communications plan should allow for feedback, as the best suggestions often come from those who are being directly impacted by the changes. We generally ask whether people have heard what they need to know about a project, whether they believe the messages they've received, and whether they have ideas for improving all Program activities.

A company spending six figures on communications during their SAP implementation assumed they were getting through to their manufacturing workforce. Our initial RQ reading suggested otherwise. Communications were described by front line personnel as "official," "empty," "eyewash," even worse (those words cannot be printed here). The most consistent comment voiced was "We haven't really heard anything about this so-called SAP project."

This organization is very traditional and hierarchical. Management worked in a solid brick building across the street from the manufacturing yard. Supervisors, who typically led ten to fifteen person workgroups, ruled the roost and were viewed as the only credible source for "what is really happening." Yet most SAP communications were either issued by the company's officers (via newsletters, memos, and the like) or were posted on the project website (though virtually none of the manufacturing personnel had access to computers).

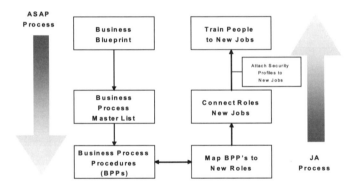

The key to retooling these communications efforts was threefold. First, we made the supervisors the primary communications channel. Second, we focused messages largely on the specific work impacts each part of the manufacturing operation should anticipate. Our "look what's coming" messages provided an effective bridge into the end-user training program. And third, we instituted a variety of "listening sessions" that afforded project and business leaders opportunities to really understand what it would take to succeed. Ultimately, though never easily, this project was a great success.

## Change Management Element #5: A Job Alignment Approach

In the simplest sense SAP defines how your organization completes transactions—how a clerk posts a credit to your general ledger, for example. In most organizations the manner in which transactions are completed is given little thought—there's a way it's done, and it's usually the way it's always been done. So confusion is a given when SAP arrives on the scene and says, in effect, there is one way and only one way any transaction can be completed (and it ain't the way you know and love).

Job Alignment eliminates this confusion by bundling transaction into SAP roles and then mapping SAP roles to existing jobs. For example, Amy Fox (a real person, but not her real name) holds the title of HR/Manager at a company implementing full-functionality SAP. Amy's current task load is diverse and demanding. "I have no clue how I'll use SAP to my job," Amy offered.

The answer was created as follows. Our team first grouped similar HR transaction into a series of HR roles with such titles as "Approval Manager" and "Benefits Processor." The role "Approval Manager," for example, comprised eleven HR transactions including "Adjust employee compensation-salary" and "Collect hourly employee time."

Our team then identified the roles Amy Fox needed to play in order to use SAP to do her HR/Manager job. In Amy's case we determined that Amy needed to adopt five SAP roles in order to be an effective, automated HR/Manager.

❑ HR001-Approval Manager

❑ HR015-Course Owner

❑ HR018-ESS User

❑ HR032-HR Professional

❑ HR057-Training Coordinator

The SAP training team was then responsible for ensuring that Amy could complete the training courses she needs to assume these roles.

But poor Amy—does the addition of five SAP roles mean she has more work than ever? If Amy thinks so I doubt she'll be a big supporter of our SAP initiative.

It shouldn't. But too often SAP Change Management programs miss one vital element: they forget to tell people the work they can STOP doing once SAP is live.

We advocate the use of a Stop/Start/Change format to transit people from existing jobs into new SAP roles. The Stop/Start/Change format is the essence of simplicity, delineating the tasks Amy can stop once SAP is Live; the tasks she must start doing within the system once SAP is Live; and the current tasks that will change once SAP is Live. Amy's Stop/Start/Change form would have 20 to 25 items, with at least half of the items tasks she can stop doing once SAP is Live. And with this knowledge we'll bid Amy adieu now and allow her to be the super-automated HR/Manager we know she can be.

## Change Management Element #6:
## A PowerUser Program

They have many names: PowerUser, SuperUser, Change Agent, Key Users. Irrespective of their labels (we will use PowerUser throughout this section) they represent an especially vital cog in your Change Management machinery.

What is a PowerUser? A PowerUser is someone who will be a daily user of your SAP system. They have expert knowledge of one or more of the processes you are automating with SAP. They are credible, well-regarded by their peers, and they can teach people new skills.

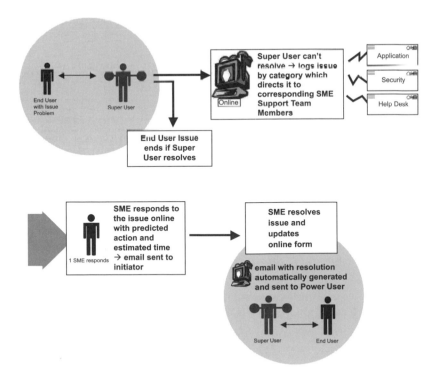

Why do you need PowerUsers? Our experience indicates that PowerUsers delivers multiple benefits:

❏ The business becomes engaged at an early stage of the project.

❏ Information flows back and forth between the project team and the business more easily.

❏ The business has a better understanding of the changes that your SAP initiative will bring.

❏ The business makes more knowledgeable decisions during the project.

❏ The business retains more internal knowledge and expertise when the project team disbands.

The size of the PowerUser Network will vary depending on 1) the size of the organization impacted by SAP, 2) the scope and complexity of the change driven by SAP, and 3) the perceived value of investing PowerUsers versus other competing program and business priorities. We typically observe that 10% to 15% of impacted personnel are tapped to be PowerUsers during an SAP implementation. PowerUsers should be selected from across the impacted organization. Given their vital role in the Blueprinting process, you should choose your PowerUsers at the project's onset. And the Program team should choose your PowerUsers; if left to the business you are likely to get the resources the business can spare (the B to C players) as opposed to the stars you need.

❏ What will these Supermen and Superwomen do for your SAP implementation? PowerUsers wear multiple hats over your implementation lifecycle.

❏ They serve as process experts when you develop your SAP Blueprint.

❑ They serve as process experts when you are developing your role-based training.

❑ They act as trainers during the delivery of role-based training.

❑ They are coaches and the first level of support for End Users once Live.

❑ They act as in-the-trenches advocates for your project through all phases of your SAP project.

Sponsorship for your PowerUsers works at two levels.

❑ PowerUsers will be committing time and effort to make your SAP project a success; their managers and supervisors must explicitly support these "extracurricular" efforts

❑ Steering Committee members and other key executives must be visible in their support of the PowerUsers' objectives and actions. It is top management's responsibility to ensure that managers and supervisors allow their people to effectively serve as PowerUsers. If can't or won't make the PowerUser position a true program priority then your SAP initiative is at-risk before it begins.

In most cases PowerUsers will need to commit about 15 % of their time to project related activities during the first three months of your implementation. As the implementation moves forward the time commitment will gradually increase to 100% in the two months before Go Live and for two to four weeks after Go Live. PowerUsers' numbers and time commitments will taper off as your SAP instance is stabilized, although you should plan to include a core group of PowerUsers in your ongoing SAP Center of Excellence

## Change Management Element #7:
## A Knowledge Transfer Process

It is highly unlikely you will implement your first waves of SAP alone. It is equally likely that you will fairly quickly want to grow the capability to implement, upgrade, and support SAP using home-grown resources (at some point you will tire of ensuring your local Marriott remains full of consultants). So from the time you need implementation assistance to that time you do not you must aggressively ensure your organization's future SAP capabilities through your Knowledge Transfer process.

Knowledge is the combination of information and experience that allows individuals, groups, and organizations to quickly and consistently achieve a set of outcomes. An SAP Knowledge Transfer process ensures that the organization cumulatively learns from its project implementation experience.

Fair enough, but how?

Most discussions of knowledge transfer are long on intent and short on process. Here's my attempt to put some substance around this slippery subject.

Your goal is to field a team of internal resources that have learned how to plan, configure, test, deploy and support your SAP instance(s).

Your team of internal resources will learn how to plan, configure, test, deploy and support your SAP instance(s) through formal training and hands-on, day to day cooperation with experienced, ready-to-teach implementation partners. Think of formal training as the catalyst, capable of getting the process started, and day-to-day cooperation as your sustained capability-building process.

From day one your consultants should teach, not do. Your people do; your consultants guide, lead, cajole, support. If they are not guiding (and instead doing) you have either forced unrealistic deadlines on your implementation partner(s), pushing them into panic mode in order to hit contracted deliverables, or you have chosen a partner who does not understand their primary responsibility to you (to equip you to thrive with SAP, not just install the darn thing and run straight to their bank).

It is your job to set knowledge transfer standards—how will you know that you know and can apply what you need to know to live with SAP? Ask experts, especially SAP, to help you identify what your people need to know and do at all points in your SAP lifecycle.

Set checkpoints—continually gauge the extent to which your people are confident that they know what they need to know and have the experience they need to gain. We worked with one client who, at the surface, looked like they were cruising. Offline conversations with project team members suggested otherwise. In the words of one team member, "We're all scared as heck that we have to keep the beast going once the consultants leave." Don't put your team in this position—ask regularly "Do we know what we need to know?"

Leverage diverse resources—learn SAP's hard lessons from as many people as possible, including people in other companies and industries, your vendors (especially SAP, they will be your best source for many topics), people in your company who implemented SAP elsewhere, and potentially industry analysts and experts (check first whether they have actually implemented SAP, preferably recently, more than once and not as a junior member of the team.)

Don't forget documentation. SAP tools afford excellent opportunities to document what was done, why, and what resulted. Identify, document, and understand "Lessons Learned" at key points in your implementation. And take the time to record and organize your insights; remember, if you do not write it down it is lost and forgotten.

## Change Management Element #8: Role Based Training

The chapter "Learning to Swim in the SAP Sea," thoroughly addresses the nature and costs of SAP training. I'd offer three points of experience to buttress the content of this chapter.

**Point One:** SAP training must be role-based; that means it is built around the roles developed during the Job Alignment process. It seems obvious. Roles encompass the SAP transactions your organization will use and the point of the training is to teach people the transactions they need to know. However, I have seen organizations take other paths, building "learning curriculums" around vague or misguided notions of how SAP will change their organization.

**Point Two:** SAP training is only as good as the context you create around it. SAP integrates an organization; what I do, and the mistakes I make, affects everyone downstream from me. You can teach people how to complete their transactions, but until they understand how their transactions are part of a larger set of transactions (i.e. part of a business process) it's hard for people to appreciate and embrace the individual discipline SAP requires. So before transaction training begins please give your end users a comprehensive overview of the processes being automated and where they fit into the process.

**Point Three:** SAP training is only as good as the support you surround it with. In the simplest sense, training takes personnel away from the daily grind of work; supervisors and managers must "allow" (in the worst case) or encourage their charges to participate. Once trained end-users need multiple opportunities to practice newly acquired skills in a "sandbox" or training system. And once live end-users need the encouragement and support afforded by a large, active PowerUser community.

"Hold on," you are now saying. "I've read all these things I need to do and I'm still skeptical. Couldn't we just train people to use SAP's functionality to work better, faster, and cheaper?"

Absolutely not. Training alone does not work.

To show someone what to do is not enough when an organization is prone to fight the changes foisted by SAP.

Remember, Change Management's purpose is to accelerate your receipt of benefits from your SAP investment. Training will show your people "how" to use SAP. But training alone cannot change your work environment so that people accept that work will be different going forward and that these differences are worthwhile for the organization. Training alone cannot impart the confidence people need to believe they can be part of SAP's changes with some, but not overwhelming personal sacrifice. You need the set of activities described in this chapter to credibly transit an organization onto SAP. Together, they teach people "why SAP" and "how SAP," the one-two punch you need to floor your organization's desires to continue "business as usual."

# CHAPTER 11

# Yes, You Can: SAP for Small and Medium-Sized Enterprises

❏ Preferences

❏ Myth and Magic

# Yes, You Can: SAP for Small & Medium Sized Enterprises

## Preferences

Over the past few years I have been advising a Fortune 50 firm that is now in the early stages of a complete implementation of SAP in North America which will be followed by a re-implementation in Europe and geographic rollouts across Asia and South America. More than 200 plants will be rolled out and there will be about 50,000 direct users. The project plan runs seven years.

I am also advising a firm with roughly $400 million in annual revenues that is just now going live after a six-month accelerated implementation.

Which of these firms do you believe will find SAP to be the easier fit?

Thought so.

Over the past twelve years, I have been involved in a large number of SAP implementations and have long since observed that while

SAP can bring enormous benefit to large enterprises, it is much more seamlessly implemented and deployed in small and medium-sized enterprises.

Consider the advantages that SMEs have over the giant enterprises.

| Advantages of SME Firms Compared to Large Enterprises | |
|---|---|
| **Advantage** | **Effect** |
| Smaller organizational hierarchies | Increased process agility |
| | Decreased change management issues |
| | Increased ability to consolidate data and financials |
| | Decreased roll-out requirements |
| Fewer operational sites | Lesser chance of process differences between sites |
| Less institutional inertia/resting on company tradition | Increased ability to change organization & processes |
| Less organizational complexity | Reduced business measurement complexity |

While it is always an honor to be engaged by a prestigious Fortune 100 firm, I often feel that my work is like pushing a boulder up a hill. When I work with small and medium enterprises, I have the pleasure of witnessing business transformation from blueprint to go-live and beyond on a more regular basis.

## Myth and Magic

One of the greatest impediments to small and mid-sized businesses (i.e. firms with less than $1B in annual revenues) is that, over the years, a number of myths about SAP have circulated in their market space. Further, it seems that these myths are given greater credence the lower down the revenue spectrum one goes.

These myths include:

1. SAP is geared to large organizations and does not work for small or mid-sized enterprises.

2. It takes an eternity to implement SAP

3. SAP consulting is too expensive for small & mid-sized enterprises.

4. SAP is too complex.

5. There is no ROI to an SAP implementation.

The fact is, these myths sprung up mostly in North America and are based on a combination of some highly-publicized SAP failures in the 1993 to 1999 time-frame and anxious IT people in small and mid-sized enterprises who are not keen on giving up their legacy systems.

In short, business leaders in these markets who are in search of greater business flexibility through responsive IT are given the myth-supported message of "You can't have SAP."

Winston Churchill wrote "A rumor gets halfway around the world before the truth puts its boots on." In order to enlighten these business leaders, let's go one step at a time...

### SAP is geared to large organizations and does not work for small or mid-sized enterprises

The greatest myth is that SAP is geared only to large-scale organizations. As of this writing, more than 26,000 SAP clients have annual revenues less than $1 billion. They represent 65% of the SAP installed base.

It should be noted that this particular myth exists only in the United States and may be due to the fact that the market for SAP R/3 was so overheated from 1993 to 1997 that SAP sales were concentrated upon the Fortune 500 and there were a number of struggling projects that made national press.

Further, to determine whether or not the SME market has only recently comprised 65% of SAP business, I consulted my archives and found the following graphic (on the right) in a PowerPoint of my 1998 version of an SAP Executive Seminar.

Note the addition of the bottom three rungs.

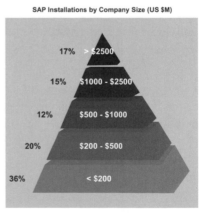

**It takes an eternity to implement SAP and SAP consulting is too expensive for small & mid-sized enterprises**

I trust that theses myths are sufficiently addressed in the sub-chapter "Accelerated SAP Implementations: A Matured View."

**SAP is too complex**

No one in his right mind would claim that SAP is not complex. By the same token, no one in his right mind would claim that an IT plant of vertically-integrated stand-alone applications that are written in a diversity of programming languages and require disparate databases is not complex.

Further, with the ascendance of NetWeaver, SAP is solving the problem of application diversity, thus reducing the complexity of firms that have SAP applications along with a high level of legacy applications and/or other enterprise applications.

**There is no ROI to an SAP implementation**

At this point, I will simply direct you back to Michael Connor's chapter on gaining business benefit.

Cut out the paragraph below and pin it to the wall. You can point it out to the next person quoting those myths.

## Yes, I can

SAP accelerated implementations are affordable. Sap is less complex than most traditional vertically-interfaced IT application clusters. SAP provides a huge support ecosystem. There is abundant evidence of measurable benefit derived from SAP. SAP works even better in small and medium-sized enterprises than it does in very large enterprises.

# Final Notes

The short version of this book:

- ❑ SAP and its eco-system are highly matured.

- ❑ SAP endeavors are business-centric and can foster business-IT alignment.

- ❑ An organization well-prepared for an SAP implementation will thrive; an ill-prepared organization will struggle.

- ❑ SAP has a shelf life of many many many years and long-term vision will be rewarded.

- ❑ If you aren't measuring, you are only rehearsing.

- ❑ "Best practices" really are "best practices." Re-invent only if it is truly necessary.

- ❑ Investment in your end users will lead to greater returns than may seem obvious.

- ❑ Change is perpetual. Embrace it.

For every phase in the SAP life-cycle, Doane Associates provides essential guidance and measurement to help clients get the most from their SAP investment.

*Business & IT Alignment/Efficiency Inventory*

We help clients through an objective self-assessment of their business and IT agility, alignment, efficiency, ecosystem, and cost management.

*SAP Executive Seminar*

This seminar informs executives and arms them with the knowledge of what SAP can do for their enterprise, how it should be implemented, how to avoid common pitfalls, and how to seize the benefits of SAP-enabled workflow.

*SAP Engagement Readiness Assessment*

This assessment assures alignment of vision and alignment of business & IT groups. It addresses the level of preparedness of leadership and project resources to successfully implement SAP according to the best practices described in this book.

*SAP Go-Live Readiness Assessment*

This assessment assures the readiness of end users to operate efficiently as well as the readiness of client staff to maintain the software and enhance business processes.

*SAP Maturity Assessment*

This assessment measures the stability of SAP applications, the competence of end users, and the client's capacity to adapt to business changes & gain measurable business value.

Contact Michael Doane at (678) 364-1788 or via e-mail at michael@michaeldoane.com

**Michael Doane** has 34 years of business and information systems experience, including sixteen years in project management on a worldwide basis. From 2001 to mid-2005, he was an industry analyst with META Group where he created and led the Professional Services Strategies group with a focus on systems integration. Before returning to SAP consulting in mid-2007, he founded Performance Monitor where he led studies of the best practices for ERP, CRM, and Outsourcing engagements based on input from thousands of clients. He is widely published (including four books on SAP) and has led more than sixty executive seminars on enterprise applications strategies and best practices. He can be reached at michael@michaeldoane.com

**Paul Reynolds** has fifteen years of primary market research experience. He advises clients using an objectives-based research approach to ensure successful project results, and has successfully managed more than 1,000 primary research projects.

Prior to co-founding Performance Monitor, Paul was the Vice President in charge of META Group's Quantitative Research Services. In this capacity, Mr. Reynolds had central responsibility for META Group's North American primary research activities as well as leadership of two of META Group's quantitative data services, including METAspectrum and a new continuous research program targeted to IT Vendors and investment research firms.

**Mike Connor** is founder and CEO of Meridian Consulting (www. meridian-us. com).

Founded in 1993, Meridian provides ERP Program Advisory support to organizations planning, implementing, and gaining benefit from ERP technologies. Meridian has supported an unparalleled diversity of ERP initiatives. It authored the Change Management elements of SAP AG's ASAP and Global ASAP Road maps.

Prior to founding Meridian, Michael was a partner with Echelon Consulting, a process improvement consultancy, was founder and Managing Director of Charlesbank Ventures, a consultancy specializing in the commercialization of new technologies, and was a founding member of PriceWaterhouse's Strategic Consulting practice.

# Ordering Information

This book is not available in bookstores.

**Direct Order:**

Send a fax to (678) 364-0137 or
an e-mail to michael@michaeldoane.com

*Provide:*

- Your Name
- Business Name (optional)
- Your purchase order number (if applicable)
- Delivery Address
- Invoice Address (if other than delivery address)
- Delivery Method (Standard mail, FedEx, other)
- Quantity Ordered
- Phone (for assured delivery)
- E-mail

Standard delivery is ground UPS. You will be billed separately by mail.

**Phone Order:** call (678) 364-1788

**Order Online:** www.sapbluebook.com
ISBN: 978-1-57579-342-9